St John's
Methodist Church
Allestree

THE
BEATITUDES

THE
BEATITUDES

GEORGE HUNSINGER

Paulist Press
New York / Mahwah, NJ

Library of Congress Cataloging-in-Publication Data

Hunsinger, George.
    The Beatitudes / George Hunsinger.
        pages cm
    Includes bibliographical references.
    ISBN 978-0-8091-0614-1 (cloth) — ISBN 978-0-8091-4887-5 (alk. paper) — ISBN 978-1-58768-394-7 (e-book)
    1. Beatitudes. I. Title.
    BT382.H84 2015
    226.9`306—dc23

                                                                    2014004361

ISBN 978-0-8091-0614-1 (hardcover)
ISBN 978-1-58768-394-7 (e-book)

Published by Paulist Press
997 Macarthur Boulevard
Mahwah, New Jersey 07430

www.paulistpress.com

Printed and bound in the
United States of America

CONTENTS

Dedicated with thanks to
Fr. Gerald O'Collins, SJ,
Teacher, Mentor, Friend

PREFACE

ALTHOUGH I FOUND IT VERY REWARDING to write this book, it was not a book I expected to write. It could almost be said that I did not choose it, but it chose me. I never imagined that I would produce a work on the Beatitudes.

I had been invited to the 2011 *Evangelischer Kirchentag* —a large biannual Protestant convention in Germany with more than 200,000 participants from around the world—in order to receive an award for my work on the theology of Karl Barth. It was understood that I would present a scholarly paper at the award ceremony. In the end, I lectured on "Karl Barth and Human Rights."

Meanwhile, the *Kirchentag* organizers had contacted me, asking if I would also lead a "Bible study" at the convention. I felt honored to be asked. I thought, "Well, sure, I can do that. I have been leading an adult Bible study in my local congregation for over fifteen years." I imagined that I would consult a few commentaries in order to lead a small group discussion. The text assigned to me was Matthew 5:1–12, the passage that contains the Beatitudes.

A few weeks before the *Kirchentag* I received a letter asking me to send my prepared text. This perplexed me, because I had no intention of drafting a written text. A few bullet points on a note card would be more than enough for the occasion. After some fast and furious back and forth, however, it became clear that my hosts had a very different idea of what I had agreed to than I did. "Bible study" to them meant a full-fledged lecture on the Matthean passage.

At first I tried to beg off. I explained that I really had nothing in particular to say about the Beatitudes and that, in any case, there had been a misunderstanding. Couldn't they just get along without me? No, they insisted, the program was already printed, and many people were looking forward to my presentation. As my perplexity was slowly descending into panic, I reluctantly agreed to come up with something. Nevertheless, I had no idea how I could meet the expectations that were laid on me. Only about two weeks remained to meet the deadline. My remarks were to be delivered in English, but, almost like at the United Nations, they would be translated simultaneously into other languages and listened to through headsets. The translators needed to have my prepared remarks in advance.

I had just finished editing the manuscript of a book about biblical interpretation. One of the themes it developed was the challenge of reading the Bible from a center in Christ. Under duress as I was, the thought occurred to me, "What would it be like to read the Beatitudes from a center in Christ?" As I began pondering the Beatitudes one by one, I could see that each of them might be taken as an element in the self-interpretation of Jesus. In any case, whether or not this was a good idea, I had to try it. I had to produce a prepared text for the simultaneous translators, and there was precious little time in which to do it.

It was a bright sunny day in June when I entered the Dresden convention center to deliver my lecture on the Beatitudes. I stood before the largest audience I had ever addressed, consisting of about five hundred people. Many of them were young, some were older, while by their costumes they seemed to represent the far corners of the earth. Afterward, members of the audience came forward to speak with me at the foot of the podium. I received words of appreciation from a white-haired man from India, from a youth worker in Germany, and from a woman with years of experience in Christian missions and the ecumenical movement, to mention only a few. Although I had managed to cover only the first four Beatitudes, it seemed that my ideas had struck a chord.

Not long afterward, my wife said to me, "Why don't you write up the rest of the Beatitudes?" That was the fatal question that led to this book. At first, I thought, "Well, why not?" It would round out the project. It would perhaps make for a useful article somewhere. With a year's sabbatical extending before me, I supposed that I could cover the second half of the Beatitudes with the same dispatch that I had finished the first. Little did I know that my whole sabbatical would be consumed.

I had divided the Beatitudes into two parts. The first four, I suggested, were about "The Needy," while the second four pertained to "The Faithful." As I dug into the material from the standpoint of my Christ-centered interpretation, I found the second four more challenging than the first. I interpreted them, not only as exemplified by Jesus, but also as fraught with consequences for today. I had to think about the practical implications of my given themes: mercy, purity of heart, peacemaking, and last but not least, persecution. Moving outward from a center in Christ, I found myself tackling questions like nonretaliation in the face of grave moral injury, the sacraments of baptism and the eucharist, restorative justice, and the hope of universal salvation. I felt impelled to develop an overview of the history of persecutions, taking into account, not only the persecution of Christians right down to the present day, but also the painful history of persecutions by Christians, especially their persecution of the Jews.

To balance matters out, I then had to return to the first four Beatitudes. Their practical implications (or at least some of them) had to be worked out at greater length. I included new material on Christian responsibility toward the poor, both domestically and internationally. I developed a spirituality of meekness, which turned out to focus on Brother Lawrence of the

Resurrection, Thérèse of Lisieux, and Dorothy Day. I sketched a brief theology of mourning, with an eye toward the ministry of listening. Finally, I attempted to relate hungering and thirsting for righteousness to the ecological crisis, concluding with a sketch of the kind of resilient communities that might sustain us through a difficult future. Needless to say, developing these ideas demanded a lot in terms of research and time, which extended through my entire sabbatical.

Let me conclude by mentioning two goals I had in writing this book. First, I wanted it to be ecumenical in intention. As a Protestant theologian in the Reformed tradition, I wanted to write something that might be meaningful not only for Protestants but also for Roman Catholics. I wanted to see if I could draw upon my Reformed heritage in a way that Catholics might feel would make sense. I, therefore, turned not only to Protestant theologians like Barth and Bonhoeffer, but also to a range of Catholic sources, including Balthasar, Benedict XVI, and the official Catechism of the Catholic Church. Having already written an ecumenical book on the eucharist, I felt that this might be the next step.

At the same time, this new book is a modest attempt at repaying an old debt. Years ago when I was a student at Harvard Divinity School, I felt that my theological education was saved by the Jesuits, who were then stationed across the Cambridge green at Weston College. No teacher was more important to me in those days than Gerald O'Collins, SJ, to whom I dedicate this work. It is a pleasure and an honor for me to have it published by Paulist Press, the oldest and largest Catholic publisher in the United States, which has also produced a great many of Fr. O'Collins's own books.

Finally, I wanted this volume to represent the analogy of faith. Although that term has more than one meaning, I use it here to indicate a certain procedure. While it may be "out of season" in academic circles, it can never be entirely out of season, I believe, for the church. The analogy of faith, as I understand it, assumes that it is permissible to interpret the Beatitudes in Matthew by bringing in biblical material from outside Matthew. I have done this rather shamelessly, though not without a certain deliberation. From the standpoint of the faith of the church, I have assumed that there is a sufficient unity in the New Testament to warrant this sort of interpretation. While I may be criticized for it, I have tried to write from faith to faith.

George Hunsinger
Easter 2014

ACKNOWLEDGMENTS

I WOULD LIKE TO THANK THREE institutions in particular: The Union of Evangelical Churches in Germany for first starting me on this project, Princeton Theological Seminary for its generous sabbatical leave program, and the Center for Christian Thought at Biola University, where much of this manuscript was written.

I would also like to thank Deborah van Deusen Hunsinger, my wife and beloved companion, who read through the entire manuscript and made many valuable suggestions. I am also grateful to Jeffrey Skaff and Alexander DeMarco for their editorial suggestions. Mr. DeMarco also worked tirelessly in tracking down permissions for the Rembrandt illustrations. Last but not least, Katherine M. Douglass used her expertise in Christian Education to provide the Study Guide.

All Bible passages are cited from the English Standard Version, though I have sometimes modified the translation to suit the context of my point.

THE BEATITUDES

Matthew 5:2–12

2 And he opened his mouth and taught them, saying:
3 "Blessed are the poor in spirit, for theirs is the
   kingdom of heaven.
4 "Blessed are those who mourn, for they shall be
   comforted.
5 "Blessed are the meek, for they shall inherit the earth.
6 "Blessed are those who hunger and thirst for righteousness,
   for they shall be satisfied.
7 "Blessed are the merciful, for they shall receive
   mercy.
8 "Blessed are the pure in heart, for they shall see God.
9 "Blessed are the peacemakers, for they shall be
   called sons of God.
10 "Blessed are those who are persecuted for righteousness'
   sake, for theirs is the kingdom of heaven.
11 "Blessed are you when others revile you and
   persecute you and utter all kinds of evil against you
   falsely on my account. 12 Rejoice and be glad, for your
   reward is great in heaven, for so they persecuted the
   prophets who were before you."

INTRODUCTION

IN THIS BOOK, I REFLECT ON THE BEATITUDES, as found in Matthew 5:3–12, by undertaking a thought experiment. I read them in a strongly christocentric manner. If Jesus Christ is the Alpha and Omega of all things, and if he is indeed the center of the universe, then he is also the center of Holy Scripture, even if that center may often be hidden. All of Scripture somehow begins and ends in him, and he himself is directly or indirectly, and sometimes only remotely, the center in relation to which any particular passage must finally be interpreted in and for the church.

What is true of Scripture in general is also true of this celebrated passage from Matthew. Jesus is the secret center of the Beatitudes as a whole and, therefore, of each one in particular. He is finally their real subject matter, and in them he points to his own person. It is he who embodies each personal attribute, he who is truly the blessing, and he who is always the promise. The Beatitudes are thus best understood as the self-interpretation of

Jesus. As Pope Benedict XVI has written, "The Beatitudes display the mystery of Christ himself, and they call us into communion with him."[1] At the same time, they are a call to discipleship and a sign of hope for the world.

The kind of ecclesial, christocentric reading that I adopt does not rule out other, more standard forms of exegesis and interpretation. Indeed it presupposes them. Any biblical text needs to be read first of all in its own immediate context and in its own particular terms, whatever they may be. Only on that basis, after preliminary standard exegesis has been carried out, can christological interpretation be ventured.

Nevertheless, the final form of the presentation need not fall into two separate parts, first the ordinary exegesis and only then the christological elaboration. A Christ-centered interpretation of the Beatitudes can be set forth without making the standard exegesis on which it relies fully explicit. Although christological interpretation presupposes standard exegesis and learns from it, it also goes beyond it and operates according to its own inner logic. It believes that Jesus Christ, as he is attested for us in Holy Scripture, is the one word of God who establishes the total relevant context—that is, the overall framework of interpretation—within which a particular passage like the Beatitudes finally needs to be interpreted. The total relevant context is established by Jesus Christ himself, incarnate, crucified, and risen, not merely by literary, social, and historical considerations.

I proceed on the assumption that the Beatitudes as they appear in Matthew exhibit a particular structure. It is the structure of "eight plus one." If we assume that there are eight basic Beatitudes in the text, we can divide them into two groups of four. The ninth Beatitude, which deals with persecution, then functions as a conclusion that underscores the two sets of four taken as a whole. However, the conclusion obviously has special relevance to the final Beatitude of the second set, which is also concerned with persecution.

The first four Beatitudes can be seen to focus on the needy and the second four to focus on the faithful. The needy are promised deliverance, while the faithful are promised a reward. Whether the needy and the faithful represent two different groups or rather, as is more likely, two different forms of one and the same group, is a complex question whose answer will be developed as we go along.

THE NEEDY

BEFORE LOOKING AT THE FIRST FOUR Beatitudes in
detail, let us reflect on the identity of the needy. How is their
neediness to be understood? What kind of neediness is it? Is this
neediness spiritual or material or perhaps somehow both?
Furthermore, how can the needy be said to be blessed? Is their
neediness to be regarded as a blessing in itself, as if the very condition of neediness were somehow a blessing? If not, then in
what sense are the needy truly blessed? What makes it possible
for them to be blessed above and beyond their neediness, and
what form does their blessedness take?

If the needy are interpreted from a center in Christ, along
with the blessing that is promised to them, and indeed pronounced upon them, then their neediness cannot be seen as
occurring in sheer isolation, nor can their blessing be merely a
pious wish. As seen from a center in Christ, the needy and their

1

blessing are determined by Good Friday and Easter. From the perspective of faith, the needy of the first four Beatitudes are those who stand under the shadow of the cross. Furthermore, precisely as those under the shadow of the cross, they are told, implicitly, that the light of the resurrection, the light of the risen Christ, falls also and especially upon them. Those who have tasted something of the cross in the bitter experiences of their lives are secretly upheld even now by the power of Christ's resurrection from the dead, and in the Beatitudes that secret begins to be unveiled. The shadow of the cross is cast by the light of resurrection hope.

The needy are not without hope because they are not without Christ. That is the secret of their existence. Objectively, they bear indirect witness to the Crucified One, in the very form of their brokenness. Jesus by his cross has made the sufferings of the world his own. His cross embraces their sufferings along with his, the sufferings of all the needy. The needy are not without hope, because he is among them and they belong to him. It is his presence to them that makes them blessed.

His presence is the presence of the heavenly kingdom. That kingdom is now veiled except to the eyes of faith, but will one day be revealed in glory for what it is. Jesus' presence to the needy in their misery is the blessing that brings them solace even now, while also pointing them to their transcendent hope. It is the hope of peace and joy in the life of the world to come, a hope that can be tasted even now.

All this is true because there is no heavenly kingdom without Jesus, and no Jesus without the heavenly kingdom. Jesus and the kingdom are one. It is he and he alone who makes the kingdom to be what it is, and he alone who makes it worth having. The kingdom would be nothing without him, nor would he be who he is without the kingdom. When he makes himself present to the needy, he makes the kingdom to be present in and with himself. He himself is the blessing of the kingdom as promised and pronounced upon the needy.

As the Crucified who was despised and rejected, he knows the grief and sorrows of the needy as no one else possibly could; while as the One raised (or in Matt 5:1–12, yet to be raised) from the dead to new life, he has the full authority to be in himself the very blessing that he pronounces upon them. He speaks to the needy from the promised future. He reveals to them that they are not alone. He proclaims that nothing can separate them from God's love, cosmic and triumphant over suffering, whether in this life or the life to come. He himself is God with us in our suffering.

1

BLESSED ARE THE POOR IN SPIRIT, FOR THEIRS IS THE KINGDOM OF HEAVEN.

IT IS FIRST AND FINALLY JESUS who defines what it means to be "poor in spirit." It is he himself who discloses and embodies not simply poverty but extreme poverty. Although in his pretemporal state he existed in the form of God, he emptied himself of his heavenly glory, taking to himself the ignoble form of a slave, even to the point of death, and indeed to death on a cross (Phil 2:6–11).

On the cross, he assumed into his very being a place of unparalleled personal impoverishment. He took his place amidst the lowliest of the low, the neediest of the needy, and the most humiliated of the shamed. He abased himself in obedience to God for the sake of the world. He showed the world his greatness through his self-humiliation.

5

He became as one who had nothing, was nothing, could do nothing, and had need of all things. He entered in that way into nothingness. He surrendered himself wholly to God for the good of others, for the good of all the needy in their own special forms of neediness, and he did so freely in absolute dependence upon God.

As one who was poor in spirit, Jesus was helpless, he made himself to be helpless, in the midst of rejection, dishonor, and death. His hope was in none other than God. At the nadir of his self-humiliation, hanging naked from the cross, he could only cry out, "My God, my God, why have you forsaken me?" (Mark 15:34).

WHO ARE THE POOR IN SPIRIT?

No one else will ever be poor in spirit in the same way as Jesus, but many others are also poor in spirit, and have been poor in spirit, in a way that reminds us of him. Who are the poor in spirit? Who are the many others alongside him?

Some would say that "the poor in spirit" must be defined as a restricted group. The context in Matthew in which the Beatitudes are presented might seem to require that the category of "the poor in spirit" belongs only to those who follow Jesus in discipleship. If so, then the only persons who could be poor in spirit would be men and women of faith. Only the faithful could be poor in spirit in conformity to Christ.

In his great discussion of the Sermon on the Mount, Dietrich Bonhoeffer seems to endorse some such view. Jesus is speaking, he observes, to his disciples. "He is speaking to those who are under the power of his call."[1] Those who follow Jesus are necessarily different from those who live according to the ways of the world (109). The community of the Crucified, Bonhoeffer suggests, consists in the community of faith (ibid.), and it seems to consist only in them. Nothing is affirmed about the neediness of the needy outside the community of faith. The needy whom

Jesus blesses in the Beatitudes would seem to be restricted to the faithful alone.

There is something unsatisfying about this view, even though it is not entirely wrong. Bonhoeffer and many others are correct to assume that the poor in spirit in this Beatitude are primarily those who have accepted Jesus' call to discipleship. It is they who are given a share in his poverty. It is they who through him know and believe that they are totally dependent on God, trusting in his care to meet all their needs. It is they who know that they can only turn to God again and again with empty hands.

Furthermore, it is they who know what the world does not yet know, namely, that those who call upon the name of the Lord will be saved. This is the knowledge that the faithful have learned, and must continually relearn, through their obedience to the gospel, wherever it may lead them. For obedience means that they will somehow be led, as Bonhoeffer saw, "to participate in the sufferings of God in the world."[2] In their discipleship to Christ, the poor in spirit do not shrink back from death, but enter into death and, in the midst of death, persevere. That is their life in the Spirit.

Nevertheless, it seems that the category of the "poor in spirit" cannot be restricted exclusively to this group. They are, to be sure, the inner circle whose center is Christ. They are the ones who know him. It is they who receive the power of his resurrection as they share in his sufferings, whatever form their sufferings may take (Phil 3:10). They rejoice in the fellowship of these sufferings as a gift of grace (Acts 5:41). They count all things as loss for the sake of knowing Christ Jesus their Lord (Phil 3:8).

But is there not also another group, found in another circle, an outer circle, whose center is also constituted by Christ? Are there not two circles here, concentric to one another, an inner circle of those who know Christ, and an outer circle of those who do not yet know him? Are not all those who are poor in spirit, in whatever form, included within one or another of these two circles? Has not the Crucified entered into solidarity with them all, the poor in spirit who know him, and the poor in spirit who do not yet know him? Is he not also objectively present to the latter group as well as being subjectively present to the former? Do not all the poor in spirit stand in solidarity with him, because he has made them his own? Does he not embrace them all in his suffering love?

JESUS AS BLESSING AND PROMISE

The blessing that Jesus pronounces upon the poor in spirit is a promise of reversal and deliverance. It is a blessing that announces to the poor in spirit that they are not forgotten by God. Because Jesus is present to them, they have a hope beyond every impulse to despair.

The blessing by which they may live even now is certainly a condition, but even more it is a relationship. The poor in spirit are blessed because God remembers them in Jesus Christ. In and through him their sufferings will be reversed into joy. Through him they will be delivered from humiliation, hopelessness, and the finality of death. Because he lives, they will live also (John 14:19).

The kingdom of heaven is not only his, but theirs. In Jesus, the blessing and the one who blesses are one. He is the promise who comes to them all.

THE POOR IN SPIRIT AND THE POOR

The poor in spirit who adhere to Christ are those who know before God that they are spiritually poor in themselves, and that they must therefore turn to God again and again. As Martin Luther stated in his last written words, "We are beggars: this is true." (*Wir sind bettler. Hoc est verum.*)[3] Being spiritually poor involves a social orientation and direction. When Jesus, though he was rich, became poor for our sakes, he made himself one with the poor and oppressed, not simply with those made destitute by sin (which of course includes all people). In him the spiritual cannot be disconnected from the material.

All persons are objectively poor in spirit, but not all are followers of Christ. Those who do follow him have a social obligation to the poor, simply because they are devoted to the One who cares for the needy in all their needs, the material as well as the spiritual. To the extent that Christ's followers may not be materially poor but command some measure of the world's resources, they have a clear mandate: defend the poor and fatherless; do justice to the afflicted and needy. Rescue the weak and needy; deliver them from the hand of the wicked (Ps 82:3–4). If anyone has the world's goods and sees his brother in need, yet closes his heart against him, how does God's love abide in him (1 John 3:17)?

Those in the developed world of relative abundance, therefore, have a special responsibility toward those in the majority world of poverty and destitution. They have a responsibility to grapple with the glaring disparities of social injustice. For the kingdom of heaven as promised by Jesus is not merely a distant ideal; nor is social reality to be defined merely by the reign of injustice and death.

The proper distinction, theologically speaking, is not between the real and the ideal, but between the real and the unreal. Only the kingdom of heaven determines what is truly real, because only the kingdom enjoys ultimate reality before God. The world of sin, poverty, and death represents the unreal world that is destined to pass away. In Christ it has passed away. In him the real world of the kingdom already belongs to the literal poor as well as to the poor in spirit. That is the essential meaning of the first Beatitude.

It seems, then, that not all the poor are "poor in spirit" in the sense of knowing by grace of their spiritual poverty. Nor have all the poor in spirit, who do know of their spiritual poverty, made solidarity with the material poor a priority. But in Christ the two are joined, and in principle they are already one. In him all persons are invited to see themselves as poor in spirit before

God; and in him those conscious of being poor in spirit are obligated to promote social justice on behalf of the literal poor.

Many of those who through Jesus are conscious of being poor in spirit, though not all, now dwell in the majority world of poverty and death. A significant but perhaps smaller number live in the world of development and abundance. Between these basic realities—the worlds of material poverty and abundance, and the spiritual conditions of the poor and the poor in spirit—there are varying degrees of complex overlap. It is an overlap that those in the world of abundance are especially called to take to heart.

Jesus is himself the promise to the poor that they are not forgotten by God and that their day of vindication is coming. Many of the literal poor already know this truth and live by it in difficult circumstances. When the literal poor are not remembered by those who through Jesus are conscious of being poor in spirit, however, the latter place themselves in spiritual jeopardy, regardless of where they may live. They are in danger of being forgotten by God, even as they have forgotten the poor. That would be one of the uncomfortable truths in Jesus' parable about the Rich Man and Lazarus (Luke 16:19–31).

Perhaps the best way for those in Christ who are conscious of being poor in spirit not to forget the literal poor would be to enter into actual contact with them. They would then see how harsh are the conditions in which the vast majority live and die. They might then be more inclined to do what can be done to alleviate those conditions, even at the cost, if need be, of some of their own privileges, or false privileges.

Church programs to bring the privileged into contact with the poor—where the literal poor and the poor in spirit from both sides might better come to know each other—would be welcome. Some such programs already exist, of course, but they are not enough and need to be strengthened. The church of the poor in spirit might then join forces with the church of the literal poor to show more truly what it means for the church to be the church in an unjust world.

Being the church demands a responsible use of money, power, and resources. Entering into face-to-face contact with the literal poor might help to stimulate greater motivation to alleviate poverty, but contact alone is not enough. It could raise consciousness and touch hearts—an essential start—but it would always need to be followed by responsible action.

THE SCOPE OF POVERTY TODAY

The human face of poverty today involves more than simple statistics, but even the statistics are troubling.[4]

- At least 80 percent of humanity lives on less than $10 a day.
- More than 80 percent live in countries where income differentials are widening.
- 22,000 infants and children die each day because of poverty, according to UNICEF. And they "die quietly in some of the poorest villages on earth, far removed from the scrutiny and the conscience of the world. Being meek and weak in life makes these dying multitudes even more invisible in death."[5] Many die of infectious diarrhea caused by contaminated water and related preventable conditions. Diarrhea is the leading cause of death among the developing world's children.
- More than one-quarter of all infants and children in developing countries are estimated to be underweight or stunted. The two worst regions in this regard are South Asia and sub-Saharan Africa.
- If current trends continue, the UN Millennium goal of halving the proportion of underweight children by 2015 will be missed by thirty million children, largely because of slow progress in the regions mentioned.

The vast majority of the world's population suffers from lack of clean water, inadequate sanitation and hygiene, and an inferior diet. This ocean of misery, hidden in plain sight, goes largely ignored by the affluent world. The better-off know little of how "the other half" dies.

Statistics for the United States, furthermore, indicate that for many Americans, the land of plenty remains a distant dream. Majority World conditions, such as those in some of the world's most deprived areas, exist within our own borders.[6]

- In 2010, more than 15 percent of all persons in America lived in poverty. The poverty rate in that year was the highest since 1993.
- Infants and children represent a disproportionate share of America's poor. They are 24 percent of the total population, but 36 percent of the poor population. In 2010, more than sixteen million children were poor.
- Extreme poverty—defined by the World Bank as households living on less than $2 a day—has more than doubled in the United States since 1996. The extremely poor struggle to survive on essentially no income at all. As of 2011, nearly 1.5 million American households, with about 2.8 million children, were suffering from extreme poverty.
- The United States has fallen from being among the top in life expectancy and infant mortality to ranking at or near the bottom among developed nations. Of the thirty nations in the OECD, only five—Mexico, Turkey, and three former Soviet bloc countries—consistently rank below the United States on such indicators.

The wide disparities in the world's assets should not go unmentioned. In the most comprehensive study of personal wealth ever undertaken,[7] a report was issued in 2006 showing "that the richest 1% of adults alone owned 40% of global assets in the year 2000, and that the richest 10% of adults accounted for 85% of the world total. In contrast, the bottom half of the world adult population owned barely 1% of global wealth."[8] In short, the top 1 percent owns 40 percent of the world's wealth; the top 10 percent owns 85 percent; and the bottom 50 percent owns only 1 percent; a sobering statistic, indeed.

Nevertheless, the situation is not necessarily as bleak as it might seem. According to the Global Poverty Project, in the last thirty years, the proportion of the world's population that lives in extreme poverty has been cut in half—from 52 percent in 1980 to 25 percent today.[9] Systemic change for the world's extreme poor is possible through educational efforts, organized campaigns, and individual actions for change.[10]

Because of the magnitude of the problem, however, initiatives by citizens, churches, and nongovernmental organizations, while indispensable, will not be enough. Large-scale structural changes are needed in the prevailing economic system or systems, so that these disastrous social results are not perpetuated. Church people who get involved at a personal level—as for example in a local soup kitchen or a hunger action program—often start asking larger questions, which can bring challenges of their own. "When I give food to the poor, they call me a saint," wrote Dom Hélder Câmara. "When I ask why the poor have no food, they call me a communist."[11]

THE BIBLE ON THE POOR

The Bible contains more than three hundred verses on the poor, social justice, and God's relation to them. The Lord God who made heaven and earth is revealed as One who takes the needs of the poor to heart, who identifies with the oppressed, and who calls his people to remember them with compassion and justice.

- "Speak up for those who cannot speak for themselves, for the rights of all who are destitute" (Prov 31:8, NIV).

- "Whoever oppresses the poor shows contempt for their Maker, but whoever is kind to the needy honors God" (Prov 14:31, NIV).
- "Is not this the fast that I have choose: to loose the bonds of wickedness, to undo the straps of the yoke, to let the oppressed go free and to break every yoke? Is it not to share your bread with the hungry and to bring the homeless poor into your house when you see the naked, to cover him, and not to hide yourself from your own flesh?" (Isa 58:6–7).
- "For you know the grace of our Lord Jesus Christ, that though he was rich, yet for your sake he became poor, so that you by his poverty might become rich" (2 Cor 8:9).

This latter verse is particularly important. First, it offers a Christ-centered reason to act on behalf of the poor. Just as Christ abased himself to alleviate our poverty before God, so in turn we are called to act on behalf of the poor in witness to him. We are to honor the grace we have received by acting generously toward others in need. We are to treat them as we, by grace, have been treated with compassion by God. Otherwise we would be thankless servants.

Second, this verse appears in a passage where Paul is discussing his apostolic collection. He appeals to the Corinthians to contribute financially, as they had promised, to the poor of the Jerusalem church. He presented his collection to them in *ecumenical* and *sacramental* terms.

Ecumenically, according to Paul, the collection was a matter of *koinōnia* or fellowship (2 Cor 8:4). It expressed the spiritual bond of peace in Christ by which all believers, Gentile and Jewish, were one. The collection was meant to forestall the spread of fatal divisions in the church.

Sacramentally, furthermore, the collection was a matter of *eucharistia* or thanksgiving (2 Cor 9:11). It was an act of gratitude on the part of the Gentile Christians for the grace they had received through the outreach of the Jerusalem church. Paul conceived of the collection in eucharistic terms as an expression of material spirituality.

The financial gift itself was seen as an embodiment of grace, the cash as a veritable sacrament of *koinōnia* (2 Cor 9:13). Eucharistic fellowship with the Jerusalem poor was embedded in this concrete, material gift. As with "the sacraments" (as they were later called), so also with the collection, for this collection was meant to effect what it symbolized (*koinōnia*) and to symbolize what it effected (*eucharistia*). Abstract expressions of fellowship were not enough.

PRACTICAL IMPLICATIONS FOR TODAY

Might not some version of the Pauline collection be revived by the churches today? Could not a new collection be designed with ecumenical breadth (*koinōnia*) and sacramental depth (*eucharistia*)? Might Protestant congregations organize relief efforts for impoverished Roman Catholics around the world, while Roman Catholic congregations reciprocated in kind by doing the same for Protestants?[12] Years ago Oscar Cullmann, the distinguished New Testament scholar, made this proposal. It would be, he suggested, a collection for the poor in order to realize the unity of a divided church.

Other strategies, some of which already exist, might also be implemented, or implemented more fully. What about "sister church" programs that pair particular congregations in affluent circumstances with majority-world congregations living *in extremis*? Such programs, which exist but need to be expanded, could be devised internationally, but they might also be implemented domestically, or even across town in a particular locale. Face-to-face contact through such a program could be key in generating the urgently needed motivation.

What about a greater use of church volunteer "work projects," again whether internationally, domestically, or even locally, that would meet the concrete needs of the poor in particular ways? What about greater support for already-existing church relief agencies like Catholic Relief Services, World Vision, Church World Service, and the Catholic Overseas Development Agency? What about increasing congregational awareness of and participation in already existing microloan projects that foster economic self-sufficiency and sustainability?[13]

Concern for the poor, of course, need not always be tightly linked with concern for the unity and well-being of a divided world Christianity, though overall both concerns are finally inseparable. Many steep challenges of transparency, accountability, cross-cultural sensitivity, and responsible administration would need to be met. But in a world where children are dying from poverty by the tens of thousands each day, almost anything would be better than indifference.

HONORING CHRIST THROUGH THE POOR

It is Jesus who blessed the poor in spirit, and it is he himself who is their blessing. What makes them blessed is precisely his presence to them. Though his presence is now hidden, it will not remain so forever, but one day will be openly revealed. "As you did it to one of the least of these..., you did it to me" (Matt 25:40). Jesus and the poor are one, for he has entered into their plight and embraced it as his own. In and through him their sorrow will one day be no more.

A great reversal is therefore at hand. In and through Christ, the last will be first, the first will be last, and all things will be made new. That is the promised future, as inaugurated by Jesus' resurrection, the future of the kingdom of heaven.

For the time being, this great reversal is to be proclaimed and practiced by Christ's followers, whom he had made conscious of being poor in spirit. The promised future needs to be declared by faith and practiced in advance through works of justice and love. The spirit of justice and love, as informed by the promised future, means honoring Christ through the poor.

BLESSED ARE THOSE WHO MOURN, FOR THEY SHALL BE COMFORTED.

JESUS IS SUPREMELY THE ONE who mourns. He mourns chiefly over the sins of the world, but also over the misery by which it is accompanied. We see the first, for example, in his lament over Jerusalem, and the second in his grief about the death of his friend Lazarus. They both are said to have moved him to weep.

Recall how Jesus mourned over Jerusalem.

> O Jerusalem, Jerusalem, the city that kills the prophets and stones those who are sent to it! How often would I have gathered your children together as a hen gathers her brood under her wings, and you would not! (Matt 23:37)

And when he drew near and saw the city, he wept over it, saying, "Would that you, even you, had known on this day the things that make for peace! But now they are hidden from your eyes" (Luke 19:41–42)

Note that Jesus' tears are being shed for Jerusalem, symbolically the holiest of cities. If even Jerusalem slays the prophets and stones those who are sent to it, if even Jerusalem does not know the way of peace, what hope can there possibly be for the world? Jesus mourns for a blinded and violence-prone city that does not know how to mourn for itself.

Jesus wept (John 11:35). He wept with those who were weeping. The news had reached him that Lazarus had died. "When Jesus saw [Mary] weeping, and the Jews who had come with her also weeping, he was deeply moved in his spirit and greatly troubled" (John 11:33). Jesus wept with the tears of a mourning God for a world filled by misery and death. In weeping for Lazarus as a particular person, and with the friends and family who had loved him, he wept for the condition of our whole sorry race. He was "a man of sorrows and acquainted with grief" (Isa 53:3).

Jesus not only mourned with those who mourned, but also with those who ought to have mourned but did not. He mourned for them all, and with them all, and even also against them all, for their sakes. He mourned because they believed more in death than in God.

WHO ARE THOSE WHO MOURN?

Those with whom and for whom Jesus mourns may again be divided into two groups. In the inner circle are those who know him as the one who mourns. They are the ones who know with Pascal that "Jesus will be in agony until the end of the world; and we cannot sleep during this time" (Pascal, *Pensées*, #553). They themselves are given a share in the mourning of Jesus. Their mourning bears witness to his, even though it is only a pale reflection of his. Like the disciples in the Garden of Gethsemane, they are prone to fall asleep while Jesus prays for them and all others in his anguish. Nevertheless, they learn through their union with him to mourn for their own sins, for the sins of the world, and for the misery of the world. Learning to mourn properly with Jesus is a mark of true discipleship.

In the outer circle, on the other hand, are those who mourn without yet knowing the mourning of Jesus. They are acutely aware of their grief (as are those in the first circle), of their personal sorrows, of their irreversible losses, whether through the death of someone they have loved, or for some ruin they have suffered, or for any other significant bereavement. They are not yet inclined to mourn for their own sins. Nevertheless, their mourning, too, finds its center and hope in Jesus, in Jesus as the one who mourns.

Because Jesus mourns with them and for them and also against them, whether they are in the inner or the outer circle, their mourning is not without hope.[1] They will be comforted. And because they will be comforted, they are already blessed, whether they know it yet or not. The mourning of Jesus—his profound sympathy and empathy for them all—is both the blessing they receive in the present and the promise of reversal and deliverance in the age to come.

JESUS AS AGAIN THE BLESSING AND THE PROMISE

Those who mourn are blessed, for it is promised that they shall be comforted [paraklēthēsontai] (Matt 5:4). Jesus Christ himself is this blessing and promise. If he is for them, though they may break his heart, who can be against them? He brings comfort to those who mourn through the gift of the Holy Spirit. The Holy Spirit is the Comforter [paraklētos] (John 16:7), who, as Athanasius said, is always in the Son, so that when the Son is given, the Comforter is always given with him.[2] It is this Comforter who is promised to those who mourn. He is the Spirit who proceeds from the Father through the Son. In and through Jesus, this Comforter is to be theirs, both now and forever. The Jesus who mourns with those who mourn brings them the Comforter, by whom they shall be comforted indeed.

Being poor in spirit in faithfulness to Jesus means learning to mourn deeply for one's sins without being overwhelmed by them. It means adopting as one's own the words once uttered by Peter: "Depart from me, for I am a sinful man, O Lord" (Luke 5:8). It means recalling the words of the Psalmist: "O LORD, pardon my guilt, for it is great" (Ps 25:11).

Beyond all mourning, however, it means trusting in the strong hand of Jesus that reached out to save Peter from drowning (Matt 14:31). It means taking to heart the message that seems too good to be true, namely, that "Christ Jesus came into the world to save sinners" (1 Tim 1:15). It means believing that there is more grace in God than sin in us. Those who mourn for their sins and repent of them will receive the surprising comfort of the Spirit through Christ. No sin is so great that it is beyond forgiveness by God. "Come to me, all who labor and are heavy laden, and I will give you rest" (Matt 11:28).

PRAYERS OF PENITENCE AND CONFESSION

Jesus promises rest to all who come to him with their burdens. At the same time, he offers them a share in his own burdens. Participating in the sorrows of Christ begins with sorrow toward oneself. One's heart of stone is replaced with a heart of flesh. One can no longer remain callous or indifferent toward one's own sins. One sees the grief that they have caused not only to others but to God. Even one's own sins by themselves, it is seen, would be enough to place Jesus on the cross.

Confessing our sins may be difficult, but not confessing them is even more difficult. Confession brings relief from an unbearable burden. It frees us not only from self-deception but also from our attempts to deceive others. Confession is an acknowledgment that we cannot deceive God.

The possibility of confessing our sins should not be taken for granted. It is a gift from above. Confession is only possible because of the mercy that covers all our sins. Through confession we receive grace to forgive ourselves as we have already been forgiven in Christ. The worst we may have done can be named and put behind us because of an ineffable forgiveness.[3]

> Blessed is the man against whom the LORD counts no
>   iniquity,
>   and in whose spirit there is no deceit.
> For when I kept silent, my bones wasted away
>   through my groaning all day long.
> For day and night your hand was heavy upon me;
>   my strength was dried up as by the heat of
>   summer.
> I acknowledged my sin to you,
>   and I did not cover my iniquity;
> I said, "I will confess my transgressions to the Lord,"
>   and you forgave the iniquity of my sin.
>
> (Ps 32:2–5)

Confession and contrition go together. Confession in words must be matched by contrition in the heart. Neither, however, is finally enough. Confession and contrition, as important as they are, must also be accompanied by the appropriate action. The general name for this action is repentance.

Although repentance is a lifelong task that can take many forms, perhaps one of its relatively neglected forms is the work of compensation. Repentance not only means intending to live a new life in the future. It also means acting, as far as possible, to compensate for damage we may have done in the past (cf. Luke

19:8). Our acts of compensation bear witness to the mystery of Christ, by whom all our debts against God have been removed by an incalculable expenditure of grace.

Those who mourn are blessed. They are blessed when they mourn for their own sins before God. They are further blessed when their mourning extends outward to encompass a deeper sensitivity for the sins and misery of the world. Above all, those who mourn are blessed, because in their sorrows, intensive and expansive as they may be, they are not alone. The Jesus who mourns with us, and for us, and against us, is the Jesus who shares fully in our sorrows in order to make all things new.

PRAYERS OF LAMENT

Prayers of lament give form to emotions of grief, mourning, and loss that might otherwise remain chaotic and formless. They cry out to God against experiences of suffering that are beyond all human explanation. They are a form of protest to God and against God that nevertheless refuses to give up on God. They see God as the One who could and should have prevented the suffering while still clinging to God for deliverance and help. Lament refuses to let go of the inscrutable God who seems to have turned away from those who mourn.

> Prayers of lament arise *in extremis*. When the people of God undergo trial and cry out for deliverance, lament is faith's alternative to despair. It is a peculiar form of petitionary prayer, one that springs from unrelieved suffering. When healing fails, lament is the hopelessness that refuses to give up hope. When injustice prevails, lament is the protest that digs in for the long haul. When humiliation abounds, lament is the self-respect that cries out to a hidden God, "How long, O Lord?" Lament bends anguish and anger into ardent supplication. Sometimes it is no more than an inarticulate cry.[4]

The most formative events in the Bible are captured by the terms *exodus* and *resurrection*. In the Old Testament, *exodus* signified the liberation of Israel from the bitter reality of slavery in Egypt. In the New Testament, *resurrection* was the inconceivable reversal that transformed the cross from disgrace into joy. All the Old Testament narratives of deliverance, as epitomized by the exodus, were fulfilled and exceeded by the empty tomb and the forty days. These primal experiences of deliverance in the midst of hopelessness left their mark on the genre of biblical lament.

Lament presupposes, paradoxically, that those who suffer are heard by God when they cry out to him. It sees suffering as something to be brought before God. In spite of everything, the ultimate purpose of lament is not protest but supplication. However anguished the protest may be, the dying embers of hope and expectation are not allowed to be extinguished. The God of the exodus and the resurrection is a God who will deliver those who mourn in his own appointed time.

The biblical psalms of lament display a certain structure. They never simply stop with lamentation. In one way or another, they involve five elements: (1) an address to God, (2) an expression of lamentation, (3) a confession of trust in God, (4) a petition to God, and (5) a vow of thanks and praise. Lament is never divorced from a renewed sense of expectation and hope.[5]

These elements can be seen, for example, in Psalm 13.

- An address to God: "How long, O LORD?" (v. 1).
- An expression of lamentation: "Will you forget me forever? How long will you hide your face from me? How long must I take counsel in my soul and have sorrow in my heart all the day? How long shall my enemy be exalted over me?" (vv. 1–2).
- A confession of trust in God: "But I have trusted in your steadfast love; my heart shall rejoice in your salvation" (v. 5).
- A petition to God: "Consider and answer me, O LORD my God; light up my eyes, lest I sleep the sleep of death, lest

my enemy say, 'I have prevailed over him,' lest my foes rejoice because I am shaken" (vv. 3–4).

- A vow of thanks and praise: "I will sing to the LORD, because he has dealt bountifully with me" (v. 6).[6]

The same five elements can be found in Psalm 22, the very psalm that was invoked by Jesus from the cross: "My God, my God, why have you forsaken me?" (22:1). After the other four elements are expressed, we again find a vow of thanks and praise: "I will tell of your name to my brothers; in the midst of the congregation I will praise you" (v. 22). The crucified Jesus mourned with those who mourn in order that they too might share in his ultimate rejoicing.

> In his Passion Jesus himself prays the psalms of lamentation. When he offered himself up on the cross in that perfect act of worship, he presented to the Father the psalms of lamentation that Israel had prayed for a thousand years, and in those psalms were the cries of all humanity.[7]

Because Jesus did not lament in vain, all those who mourn are blessed in him and by him. Because he was delivered from the grave, they too shall be delivered and comforted. Jesus, crucified and risen, is the blessing and the promise held out to those who mourn.

THE MINISTRY OF LISTENING

Being poor in spirit—as embodied in those who mourn, and as embodied in those who know that in Christ their mourning has been shared and heard—involves learning how to hear and comfort others. It means learning that God "comforts us in all our affliction, so that we may be able to comfort those who are in any affliction, with the comfort with which we ourselves are comforted by God" (2 Cor 1:4). This ministry of comfort is largely a ministry of being present in a supportive way. It is a ministry of caring, of listening, and of trusting the silences. It is an active ministry in which one asks a bereaved or grieving person if something is troubling them, in which one expresses concern, and in which one listens to and validates what is said. Help is offered when appropriate, but responsible decisions of the grieving person are supported.

In this ministry, we do not just wait for the grieving person to take the initiative, but instead reach out. A policy is adopted in which we refrain from judging or blaming, from applying pressure, and above all from giving advice. We simply try to be present in openness and love, encouraging the person to mourn all the losses he or she has endured. For that is how Christ, and those faithful to him, will have brought comfort to us in our own times of mourning. "Cast your burden on the LORD, and he will sustain you" (Ps 55:22). "[Cast] all your anxieties on him, because he cares about you" (1 Pet 5:7). Bringing a measure of comfort to those who mourn is a foretaste of the deliverance to come.

The ministry of comfort includes a social and political dimension. No victim of injustice—whether it be from torture, racial persecution, sexual abuse, or some other comparable trauma—can recover by ignoring what occurred. The only way such victims can move forward is by looking back to heal what is wounded in their past. There is much moral reckoning that needs to be worked through. Anger, grief, and shame need to be transformed into positive sources of action and renewal. Trauma victims tell us that trauma cannot be healed unless it is acknowledged, validated, and invested with moral significance. In this process, the ministry of comfort is no substitute for social change, but it is nonetheless a good in itself as well as a possible means to that larger end. The comfort promised by Jesus is finally communal, not just individual, in scope.

A friend, who has organized a particular ministry of listening, writes,

> Among the least listened to people in the world are the
> homeless. These are some of the most lectured to, preached

at, cursed at, and ignored people you will ever meet. Among the most dehumanizing aspects of homelessness, I have come to believe, is the ignoring: these are deeply marginalized people. It's remarkable the good you can do for a homeless friend by the simple act of listening.

Some students and I practice a weekly ministry of listening at a local Catholic Worker house. For two hours each week, we descend on the house's soup kitchen, fan out among the homeless, and do our best to listen, really listen, in a posture of quiet, warm-hearted, non-censorious love.

It took some time for people to warm to us. Many still haven't. But there are many there who see us coming, make a beeline for us, and begin to talk. And we have heard some remarkable stories indeed. There is the woman whose daughter, some years in the past, had been sexually abused by her uncle repeatedly, but was afraid to say anything about it for fear that her uncle would kill her and others in the family. Or the woman whose family disowned her because of her addictions, who had been studying to pass an insurance exam and had put her addictions behind her, and was hopeful that perhaps now her family would take her back. Or the man who had been addicted to cocaine for years but had been sober for a week and wanted prayer that he could make it another week. Or the woman filled with regret and tearfully relating that her brother had died while she was away, sunk in addiction.

Though it's hard to be sure, I think we are doing good to these brothers and sisters by listening to them as we do. I know they are doing great good to us. These are people who know first hand what it is to really depend on God. We know so little of that, operating as we do from positions of privilege and affluence. By sharing their stories, their lives, with us, they are teaching us much about what it means for God—to borrow the language of the psalms—to be one's refuge and fortress (Ps. 91:2).[8]

In a similar vein another writes,

That's the thing about dealing one-on-one with homeless people: they stop being a category—a mental abstraction, a them—and become richly complex individuals with stories as filled with virtue as with vice, but I realized as time went on that they were really bringing Christ to me. In those weary faces at the tables, I saw Christ staring back at me, asking me where I'd been all this time. He had been out there, in doorways, shivering in cold rains and stumbling in rags and singing to the midnight streets, waiting for me to show up. I feed Him in His Homelessness, and in return, in an act of astounding and tender mercy, He shows me the depths of my own brokenness.[9]

CONCLUSION

The Jesus who mourns with those who mourn, and who teaches us to mourn with him, is the same Jesus who brings the comfort that he promises, and who teaches us to comfort others with the comfort through which we are comforted by God. When we mourn with Jesus, we will join him in remorse for our sins through confession, in prayers of lament in times of desolation, and in the ministry of listening with those who sorrow and grieve. Jesus is the promise of comfort for all who mourn. His presence to us in our contrition, in our laments, and in our listening to others both attests and mediates even now the perfect comfort that is to come.

3

BLESSED ARE THE MEEK, FOR THEY SHALL INHERIT THE EARTH.

JESUS DEFINES WHAT IT MEANS to be meek. He was meek in more than one way. Certainly, he was meek in contrast to the proud, stiff-necked, and ungrateful souls who comprise our fallen race as a whole and who threaten to stain it with an indelible stain. In humility and gentleness, he undertook what no one else could do. He submitted himself without sin to the will of God, to God's harsh and dreadful love, and he did so for our sakes and in our place. He was by his own account "meek and lowly of heart" (Matt 11:29), finally surpassing even Moses, who was himself "very meek, more than all people who were on the face of the earth" (Num 12:3). He was the Lord who took the form of a servant in order to die for us on the cross.

Yet Jesus was more than exceedingly humble. At the same time, he was also humiliated. He was "despised and rejected by men" (Isa 53:3). He "came to his own, and his own people did not receive him" (John 1:11). All things had been made through him (1 Cor 8:6), yet he had nowhere on earth to lay his head (Matt 8:20). He was homeless, dispossessed and cast out, yet he did not become violent or vindictive.

> He was afflicted,
>   yet he opened not his mouth;
> like a lamb that is led to the slaughter,
>   and like a sheep that before its shearers is silent,
>   so he opened not his mouth.
>
> (Isa 53:7)

Made helpless by oppression and judgment, he was "stricken for the transgression of [his] people" and "cut off out of the land of the living" (Isa 53:8). Jesus shows us his meekness through his humility and through his entry into humiliation.

All those in the inner circle of grace—the faithful who know that in Jesus God's eternal Son took the form of humility and humiliation—are called to conform to him in meekness. "Take my yoke upon you," he urged, "and learn from me, for I am meek and lowly in heart, and you will find rest for your souls" (Matt 11:29). Those who find their rest in Jesus will count others as better than themselves (Phil 2:3). They will refrain, if need be, from insisting on their own rights. They too, in their own way, will take the form of a servant, to the glory of Christ and God the Father.

Nevertheless, they will do these things with dignity. They will resist being merely submissive and compliant. They will not allow themselves to become a doormat. They will speak out for those who are marginalized and humiliated, for those who have no rights or from whom those rights are robbed and taken away. For the faithful, the question of when to submit and when to resist is an ongoing task of spiritual discernment.

They will always strive to stand up for the silenced, the humiliated, and the abused. They will work against injustice and oppression, knowing that Jesus aligned himself with those who are humiliated in order to set them free. In the careworn faces of the abused, the humiliated, and the oppressed—in the wretched of the earth—the faithful will see the face of Jesus himself. And in the faces of the wretched, they will also see a reflection of themselves as the needy whom are embraced and delivered by him from sin and death.

In Jesus, the meek, whoever they may be, receive the promise and the blessing that they shall inherit the earth. Those who are disinherited or dispossessed will no longer be cut off out of the land of the living. Jesus allowed himself to be cut off before them in order that a limit might be set. He himself was cut off so that the wretched might be cut off no more. He is the embodied promise that the meek shall inherit the earth, that they shall receive their rightful inheritance as sons and daughters of God. He himself guarantees, by his cross and resurrection, the vision of the Psalmist, not only that "the evildoers shall be cut off," but that "those who wait for the LORD shall possess the land" (Ps 37:9).

His presence to the meek is already the blessing he pronounces. He himself is the blessing who ensures that there is no need to "fret…because of evildoers" or be "envious of wrongdoers" (Ps 37:1). He himself assures by his presence that the wicked and wrongdoers "will soon fade like the grass, and wither like the green herb" (Ps 37:2). For by him and through him the earth does not belong to them. "The earth is the LORD's and the fullness thereof" (Ps 24:1), and its blessings will be distributed in Christ.

As understood in the Beatitudes, the idea of the needy therefore has a double aspect. It involves both a spiritual attitude and a social condition. Meekness is a case in point. On the one hand, it means spiritual humility before God, while on the other hand, it means being socially marginalized, voiceless, and dispossessed. Both aspects need to be taken seriously so that neither is played off against the other, as if they were competitors. It would be a mistake to think that meekness is not a social condition but merely a spiritual attitude, just as it would also be wrong to focus on the social aspect of meekness at the expense of its spiritual dimension. The blessing and the promise, as proclaimed and embodied by Jesus, include both.

It is in and through Jesus Christ that the meek shall inherit the earth. In him they are the ultimate inheritors of the promise made originally to Abraham. The promise to Abraham of the land—"the land that I will show you" (Gen 12:1)—underwent many variations throughout the history of the covenant, until in Christ it became the promise of the kingdom. Moreover, the blessing given to Abraham was universal in scope: "In you all the families of the earth shall be blessed" (Gen 12:3). In Christ this promise is at last fulfilled for all, but only by including the one group in particular most excluded from earthly goods in this life: the meek. Universality is shown precisely by including the out-cast. This inclusion, we might say, indicates a preferential option for the meek, though it occurs on behalf of all.

Only those with a heart for the poor and needy can have a heart for God. As Bonhoeffer stated,

> The hungry need bread and the homeless need a roof; the oppressed need justice and the lonely need fellowship; the undisciplined need order and the slave needs freedom....To allow the hungry to remain hungry would be blasphemy against God and one's neighbor, for what is nearest to God is precisely the need of one's neighbor.[1]

According to Holy Scripture, God is aligned with the poor and needy against those who unjustly exploit them.

> All my bones shall say,
> "O LORD, who is like you,
> delivering the poor
> from him who is too strong for him,
> the poor and needy from him who robs him?"

(Ps 35:10)

32

For the needy shall not always be forgotten,
  and the hope of the poor shall not perish forever.

(Ps 9:18)

God "will execute justice for the needy" (Ps 140:12) and "deliver them from the hand of the wicked" (Ps 82:4). Works of mercy and justice in the present bear witness to this deliverance yet to come.

In Christ deliverance is anticipated in the form of resurrection hope. Resurrection hope is a hope for this world, not for some other world. It is a hope that this world will be transformed, not that it will be escaped. It is a hope that evil in all its forms will be utterly eradicated, that past history will be redeemed, and that all the things that ever were will be made new. It is the hope for a new creation, in which God is really glorified as God, human beings are truly human, and peace and justice reign on earth. "Behold, I am making all things new" (Rev 21:5). In Christ the meek—both the humble and the humiliated—are placed under the sign of resurrection hope.

THE SPIRITUALITY OF MEEKNESS

Three figures from Christian history may be mentioned who represent the spirituality of meekness. Although they lived in very different times, they all had at least one thing in common. They all learned to find God in the ordinary. Spiritual practices leading to holiness were for them not something restricted to a spiritual elite. They were rather available to any who chose to adopt them in their everyday lives. These practices were difficult only in their simplicity. They were grounded in meekness and devised for a democracy of holiness.

BROTHER LAWRENCE OF THE RESURRECTION (1614–91)

Brother Lawrence served as a lay brother in a Carmelite monastery in Paris. Before joining the Discalced Carmelite

Priory of Paris at the age of twenty-six, he had fought in the Thirty Years War and worked for a while as a valet, having experienced a conversion at the age of eighteen. Lacking the education to become a priest, he spent much of his life toiling in the kitchen, while in his later years, when he had more trouble standing for long hours, he repaired sandals. He was sometimes sent on expeditions to purchase a supply of wine for the priory. These assignments were not easy for him, since he had been crippled during the war and spent much of his life in nagging pain. After his death, his letters and conversations were compiled into a little book, *The Practice of the Presence of God.*[2] Translated into several languages, it has found a wide range of influence in the churches, including Quakers, Episcopalians, Methodists, Roman Catholics, and many others among its admirers.

Prayer for Brother Lawrence meant conversing with God throughout the tedious chores of the day. Every mundane task, whether peeling a potato, flipping an omelet, or washing the dishes, was done for the love of God (116). What God considered, he believed, was not the greatness of the deed but the love with which it was performed (118).

> The time of business does not differ for me from the time of prayer. Despite the noise and clatter of my kitchen, where often enough several people are asking me for different things at the same time, I possess God as peacefully as if I were kneeling before the blessed sacrament. (115, revised trans.)

Brother Lawrence conversed with God everywhere, asked God for whatever he needed, and gave thanks continually as his needs were met (40).[3]

> I keep myself in his presence by simple attentiveness and a general loving awareness of God that I call the "actual presence of God" or better, a quiet and secret conversation of the soul with God that is constant. (53, revised trans.)

The holiest, most ordinary, and most necessary practice of
the spiritual life is that of the presence of God. It is to take
delight in and become accustomed to his divine company,
speaking humbly and conversing lovingly with him all the
time, at every moment, without rule or measure, especially
in times of temptation, suffering, aridity, weariness, even
infidelity and sin. (36)

Brother Lawrence felt that anyone was capable of these
ongoing conversations with God. A brief lifting up of the heart
was enough. He believed that short petitionary prayers, simple as
they may be, were pleasing to God (107). Learning to offer
prayers continually might be difficult at first but eventually
becomes second nature:

I believe there is nothing so necessary or easy. (57)

We must not get discouraged when we forget this holy practice, for all that is needed is to calmly take it up again; once
the habit is formed we will find contentment in everything.
(106)

Strenuous methods for entering into God's presence were
unnecessary. We need only undertake everything in love to God,
offering our daily tasks to him, and calling upon him continually
for assistance. That was the daily practice of Brother Lawrence.

Two further points are especially noteworthy. First, Brother
Lawrence displayed a holy nonchalance toward his personal lapses
into sin. "In this way we will find every virtue in him [Christ] without having any of our own" (37). He felt that he had no need of a
spiritual director, but a great need for a confessor. "He acknowledged his sins and was not surprised by them," wrote a confidant.

He confessed them to God and did not plead before him to
excuse them; after that he returned to his ordinary exer-
cises of love and adoration in peace. (93)

> Without worrying, we must look to the blood of Christ for the remission of sin, working only at loving God with our whole heart. (94)

Second, Brother Lawrence was careful not to treat God as if God were merely the means to an end. God was to be desired essentially for his own sake, not as the means to some separate, external good (145). God was seen as an intrinsic good, not an instrumental value. In particular, God was to be trusted and petitioned in the midst of any suffering he might send.

> [We are] to suffer as long as he desires....Happy are they who suffer with him. Get used to suffering, and ask him for the strength to suffer as he wants, for as long as he judges necessary....Illnesses [should be received] as graces from God....[We should] regard them as coming from the hand of God....[They are] the means he uses for [our] salvation. (73)

Brother Lawrence expected that, along with all the blessings he had known, he would also receive his share of suffering and pain.

> He did not worry about it, however, knowing well that since he could do nothing by himself, God would not hesitate to give him the strength necessary to bear them. (92)

> Once when he was seriously ill, a man came to him and asked which he would choose: if God permitted, to remain alive longer to increase his merits, or to receive them now in heaven. Without deliberating, Brother Lawrence answered that he would leave the choice to God, and that as far as he was concerned, he had only to wait patiently until God revealed his will. (118)

Brother Lawrence faced death calmly and without anxiety. As he neared his end, it almost looked as if he never had a moment's discomfort, even when his illness was the most painful. Joy appeared not only on his face but even in his manner of speaking. The friars asked if he was really in pain. "Pardon me," he said, "I am in pain. My side hurts but my spirit is at peace" (121).

Saint Thérèse of the Child Jesus and the Holy Face (1873–97)

The parallels between Saint Thérèse of Lisieux and Brother Lawrence are so striking that one might think the latter had been an influence on her, especially since both were Carmelites. Conrad De Meester, however, was moved to pose the question in reverse: "If he had not preceded her by two centuries, one would think Lawrence's emphasis on merciful love and on the simplest things of each day were borrowed from his little sister."[4]

As it turns out, however, Brother Lawrence's teachings were unknown to her. None of his writings were available in the library of the Lisieux convent.[5]

Although Thérèse of the Child Jesus and the Holy Face—otherwise known as Thérèse of Lisieux—lived only to the age of twenty-four, she was not only eventually canonized as a saint, but also elevated to the rank of Doctor of the Church. Her canonization occurred in 1925, and her elevation in 1997.

She was born into a pious family, from which two sisters preceded her into convent life and two others followed.[6] Showing remarkable spiritual insight even as a small child, she received the certainty of a divine call to enter Carmel at the age of nine, and was admitted to the convent at the unheard-of age of fifteen, the usual age being at least twenty-one. Her early admission was set in motion by a fervent, almost brazen appeal to Pope Leo XIII, during an audience she had with him in Rome. At the age of twenty-three, she contracted tuberculosis, dying little more than a year later after an excruciating illness, during which she composed many of her most important writings.[7]

The writings of St. Thérèse are far more extensive, more effusive, and more intensely personal than those of Brother

Lawrence. Our attention will be restricted here to what she called her "Little Way," in which many of Lawrence's ideas would seem to be echoed and extended.

Like Brother Lawrence, St. Thérèse renounced all arduous ascetical practices as a way to holiness. She too believed in a spirituality of everyday life. She could draw no strict boundaries between contemplation and action. In this respect, Hans Urs von Balthasar believed she was "the greatest saint of modern times," in particular because she was "the first to rid contemplation of its Neoplatonic relics."[8] For St. Thérèse, fruitfulness in action, not effectiveness in spiritual ascent, was the purpose of contemplation and prayer.

St. Thérèse believed that everything in her Little Way could be imitated by others: "In my little way there are only very ordinary things; it is essential that little souls should be able to do everything I do" (270).

The epithet *little* meant bypassing extraordinary methods of mysticism and asceticism. Great mortifications were too much for her. She looked for a way of reaching heaven that offered a "perfectly straight, short and completely new little way" (84). As opposed to the traditional stairway of ascent, to be traversed by strenuous effort, she proposed an elevator.

> Now there's no more need to climb the steps of a staircase....I would...like to find an elevator to lift me up to Jesus, because I'm too little to climb the rough staircase to perfection....The elevator that must lift me to heaven is your arms, Jesus! For that I don't need to become big.[9]

Spirituality was not a matter of ascent but instead of downward mobility. Paradoxically, the only way up was down. "You are wanting to climb a mountain whereas the good God wishes you to climb down. He is waiting for you in the fertile valley of humility" (278).

Humility meant renouncing justification by works, living by faith alone, surrendering to whatever suffering God might bring, abandoning all perfectionism in order to rely solely on mercy, trusting unreservedly in God's love, and adopting a holy nonchalance toward one's constant personal failings. It meant claiming no merit of one's own, but finding it wholly in Jesus (283).

> I'm not counting on my merits, since I have none, but I hope in the One who is Virtue and Holiness Itself. It is he alone who, being content with my feeble efforts, will raise me up to himself and, covering me with his infinite merits, will make me a saint.[10]

> Faith is to be reckoned as righteousness to us also....Since it is by faith that we are justified, let us grasp the fact that we have peace with God through our Lord Jesus Christ. Through him we have confidently entered into this new relationship of grace, and here we take our stand, in happy certainty of the glorious things he has for us in the future....Now we are seeing the righteousness of God declared quite apart from the Law....It is a righteousness imparted to, and operating in, all who have faith in Jesus Christ.[11]

The resonances between Thérèse and Luther have been noted by both Balthasar and de Meester.[12] If so, then the Little Way would seem fraught with ecumenical significance. Thérèse knew herself as a forgiven sinner.

> I entrust God with my infidelities; I tell them to him in great detail, and I think in my daring trust that I achieve all the more power over his heart and draw unto myself even more of his love who is come to call, not the just, but sinners. (352)

> Even if I had committed every crime imaginable, I would still have the same trust; all these offenses would be like a drop of water falling into a glowing furnace. (350)

Her final months on earth were filled with enormous agony and pain, as she often felt she could not breathe. Though the sisters of the convent could not always perceive it in her face, her faith underwent a severe trial. In what Balthasar describes as her most extreme statement, she even allowed herself at one point to confide, "I no longer believe in eternal life; it seems to me there is nothing beyond this mortal life. Everything is brought to an end. Love alone remains" (342).

Yet her disposition, in the end, did not seem far from Brother Lawrence:

> Were our Lord to offer me my choice, I would choose nothing. I only will what he wills. (148)

> I am not worried about my future, I am sure that God will do his will, it's the only grace I desire.[13]

> I don't know when my exile will end…but finally the last night will come….I rise and go to Him in confidence and love.[14]

DOROTHY DAY (1897–1980)

Like Brother Lawrence, St. Thérèse embraced God as an intrinsic good as opposed to an instrumental value. She rejected all reductionist ideas of God, as if God were nothing but the object of personal salvation and happiness. God was to be loved, not used. Thérèse would seek nothing in God other than God himself. Love was the ultimate end by which other praiseworthy ends were included and surpassed. Yet they could all be renounced, if necessary, for the sake of a Love supreme.

An anecdote, as told by Dorothy Day, illustrates her disposition: "When her sister Celine sat reading her a [pamphlet] on eternal beatitude, suddenly Thérèse interrupted her—'It is not that which attracts me. It is Love! To love and be loved, and to return to earth to make Love loved!'"[15]

Devotion to divine love above all else was a quality that characterized Dorothy Day as much as it did Brother Lawrence and St. Thérèse. It is no accident that she was drawn to each of them. While she produced a book on the life and writings of St. Thérèse, it is not widely known that she also contributed the preface to a new edition of *The Practice of the Presence of God*.[16] She went beyond them both, however, by practicing God's presence among the working-class poor and by socializing the Little Way.

Born in Brooklyn, Dorothy Day spent her childhood moving with her middle-class parents from city to city until her father found steady work in Chicago. Though her parents were churchgoing Episcopalians, they were not the sort of high-commitment Christians that Dorothy would eventually become. Religious stirrings marked her growing-up years, but at first came to no great effect. Despite being baptized and confirmed, she regarded herself as an agnostic. Dropping out after two years of college, she moved to New York's Lower East Side in 1915, where she became a left-wing journalist writing for socialist newspapers.

The bohemian lifestyle that she adopted took on a countercultural profile that she never abandoned. She became a lifelong critic of social injustice as generated by corporate capitalism. In her personal life, she entered into two common-law marriages. An abortion, which she later regretted bitterly, marked the first. By the time she again became pregnant in the second, she was in the process of converting to Catholicism. Her conversion, along with her having refused a second abortion, eventually led to the dissolution of her second long-term relationship.

The turning point of Day's life came when she met Peter Maurin in 1932. Maurin was a self-educated French peasant who had acquired an extensive knowledge of the patristic spiritual writings, along with the social teachings of the Catholic Church. He also had a vision of how to create an alternative religious community, including voluntary poverty, houses of hospitality, a return to working the land, and the publication of a workers' newspaper. That became the program of the Catholic Worker Movement, to which Day devoted the rest of her life.

Through Day's leadership, the Catholic Worker Movement became known for a number of distinctives: its concrete involvement on behalf of the poor; its nonviolent direct action, leading to many arrests; and its outspoken pacifism, especially involving antinuclear protests. Despite uncomprehending critics, Day's life of spiritual integrity was eventually recognized for what it was. When she died in 1980 at the age of eighty-three, she was described as "the most significant, interesting, and influential person in the history of American Catholicism."[17] She received several distinguished awards during her lifetime and was proposed for sainthood by the Claretian Missionaries in 1983. The case for her canonization remains open.

Politically, Day took her bearings from anarchists like Kropotkin, whom she had read in her youth, but spiritually, she took inspiration from writers like Brother Lawrence and St. Thérèse. She read them for their relevance in difficult times.

On Brother Lawrence:

> Living today in a time of war, crying out Peace when there is no Peace, fearing age and death, pain and darkness, destitution and loneliness, people need to get back to the simplicity of Brother Lawrence,…whose "little way" makes our burdens light and rejoices the heart.[18]

> I try to practice the presence of God after the manner of Blessed Lawrence, and pray without ceasing as St. Paul advised.[19]

On St. Thérèse:

> When I lay in jail thinking…of war and peace, and the problem of human freedom, of jails, drug addiction, prostitution, and the apathy of great masses of people who believe that nothing can be done—when I thought of these

things, I was all the more confirmed in my faith in the little way of St. Thérèse. We do the minute things that come to hand, we pray our prayers, and beg also for an increase of faith—and God will do the rest.[20]

Brother Lawrence and St. Thérèse helped Day to temper her anarchism with a kind of Christian personalism. While a new society was to be created within the shell of the old, Day entertained no grandiose schemes of social revolution:

We are not expecting a utopia here on earth, but God meant things to be much easier than we have made them. A man has a natural right to food, clothing and shelter. A certain amount of goods is necessary to lead a decent life. A family needs work as well as bread....We must keep repeating these things. Eternal life begins now.[21]

One could only strive to live faithfully while leaving the outcome to God. Were such tactics as feeding the hungry through soup kitchens, offering shelter to the homeless, and getting arrested for direct action against the threat of nuclear war worthwhile? What sense did all this really make? A clue was found in St. Thérèse. "Do we see results, do these methods succeed? Can we trust them? Just as surely as we believe in 'the Little Way' which in this last century St. Thérèse Martin proclaimed and restated to the world, we believe and know that this is the only success."[22]

The only success was in methods by which conscience was not violated, and in actions, however modest, by which the indigent were treated with dignity.

I wrote the life of St. Thérèse because she exemplifies the "Little Way." We know how powerless we all of us are, against the power of wealth and government and industry and science. The powers of this world are overwhelming. Yet it is hoping against hope and believing, in spite of "unbelief," crying by prayer and by sacrifice, daily small, constant sacrificing of one's own comfort and cravings— these are the things that count....And love. All these means are useless unless animated by love.[23]

Radical politics combined with sacrificial living and the spirituality of meekness led Day to wisdom about the "paradox of poverty."

I condemn poverty and I advocate it; poverty is simple and complex at once; it is a social phenomenon and a personal matter....People do not understand the difference between inflicted poverty and voluntary poverty; between being the victims and champions of poverty. I prefer to call the one kind destitution, reserving the word poverty for what St. Francis called "Lady Poverty."[24]

Destitution was to be alleviated, while poverty could be chosen out of love for God—and for the poor as loved by God. "Those who can't see Christ in the poor," Day remarked, "are atheists indeed."[25]

CONCLUSION

The spirituality of meekness, as seen in these writers, meant relying entirely on God, calling upon God continually, and receiving all things (including suffering) as from the hand of God. It meant using one's personal suffering as a school for humility. For the crippled Brother Lawrence, it meant loving God in the midst of the ordinary, asking God each day to supply all one's needs. For the childlike St. Thérèse, it meant finding one's holiness not in oneself but in Jesus, loving him not only through the Little Way but especially in the midst of unbearable affliction. For the tough-minded Dorothy Day, finally, it meant socializing the ordinary to include the working-class poor, becoming poor oneself in order that the indigent might receive a measure of dignity, and submitting to repeated arrests that the world might turn back from the scourge of war. Each was a powerful witness to the meekness of Christ, who became poor to make many rich, and meek with all the meek, that the promise of inheriting the earth might be theirs.

4

BLESSED ARE THOSE WHO HUNGER AND THIRST FOR RIGHTEOUSNESS, FOR THEY SHALL BE SATISFIED.

IT IS JESUS, ABOVE ALL, who hungers and thirsts for righteousness. Righteousness represents not only his deepest desire but also his supreme achievement. In him we can see most clearly that righteousness has a double aspect, the one vertical and the other horizontal. Through his death and resurrection, Jesus establishes righteousness for our sakes in both dimensions. He does so vertically by destroying all human ungodliness, and horizontally by removing all human wickedness (Rom 1:18). Ungodliness is the tap root from which the lateral roots of wickedness shoot forth. Jesus attacks the lateral roots by doing away with the tap root. In restoring us to God, he restores us to one another as well.

It is against all human ungodliness and wickedness that the wrath of God is poured out from heaven (Rom 1:18). Jesus makes himself to be our righteousness (1 Cor 1:30) by bearing and removing the wrath that would otherwise fall upon us. God's wrath is the form taken by God's love against all that contradicts and opposes it. It is the divine "No" to sin, evil, and the finality of death. It is the fierce divine rejection of everything that would separate us from God and so from one another. Through the obedience of Jesus to the point of dying on the cross, our tragic negation of God's love has been met, removed, and destroyed.

Jesus himself is our righteousness, because he bears and bears away the unbearable consequences of sin for our sakes. He takes our sin and death to himself and gives us his righteousness and life. This is the great exchange (*admirabile commercium*) that forms the deepest mystery of our salvation (2 Cor 5:21). It is God's negation of our negation. In handing himself over to sin and death and rising again from the dead, Jesus saw the travail of his soul and was satisfied (Isa 53:11). He himself is the righteousness of God in whom all unrighteousness, whether vertical or horizontal, is overcome.

The faithful are called to bear witness to Christ and his righteousness. They are called to receive and proclaim the righteousness established in him. They are to do so in both dimensions, the vertical and the horizontal. They are summoned, first of all, to embody the good news in their communal lives. They are commissioned to show that in Christ our warfare with God is ended (Isa 40:2). They are especially to show this as a eucharistic community. As Bonhoeffer observed,

> They will eat the bread of true life in the future heavenly Supper with their Lord. They are blessed because of this future bread, since they already have it in the present. He who is the bread of life is among them even in all their hunger. This is the blessedness of sinners.[1]

Which of course means forgiven sinners.

Righteousness cannot be received in relation to God (vertically) unless it is also pursued in relation to our neighbors (horizontally), because faith without works is dead. The righteousness of God is therefore inseparable from the struggle for social justice. Those who enjoy God's righteousness in Christ while remaining indifferent to social injustice are unprofitable servants. They may be one reason why Luther once remarked that "the curses of the godless are sometimes more pleasing to God's ear than the hallelujahs of the pious."[2]

Those within the inner circle of grace would do well to learn from the good examples that can be found within the outer circle of those who do not yet know Christ, and who may even believe they reject him. For the outer circle, too, is centered, in its own way, in Christ. It seems that there are many who hunger and thirst for righteousness who do not yet or no longer confess him. Yet in their own way, are they too not embraced objectively, and sometimes moved to take appropriate action, by the centrality of his grace and righteousness?

Christ's righteousness is at once a promise and a blessing. Those who hunger and thirst for righteousness, in all its forms, the vertical as well as the horizontal, will find their ultimate fulfillment in him. Whether in the eucharist or in struggles for social justice or in other forms, it is the mystery of Christ's real presence as our righteousness that guarantees what the final outcome will be. In both concentric circles as centered in him, all those who hunger and thirst for righteousness, as he himself hungers and thirsts, will, like him, see the travails of their souls and be satisfied. "But according to his promise, we are waiting for new heavens and a new earth in which righteousness dwells" (2 Pet 3:13).

HONORING THE INTEGRITY OF CREATION

Today hungering and thirsting for righteousness takes on a special urgency in relation to the travail of the earth. God's good creation has been so despoiled, and continues to be so despoiled, that it is no longer clear whether our species can escape destruction. The enormity of the looming environmental crisis seems beyond our collective capacity to grasp. The earth's resources are being consumed at an unsustainable rate. Millions of tons of topsoil are being sluiced into the oceans. Underground aquifers are being drawn down. Former croplands are wasted by salinization or desertification. Fisheries are being depleted and forests overharvested, while land, water, and air are increasingly polluted with deadly toxins. The cumulative effect is enormous. Global warming promises to bring heat waves, droughts, torrential flooding, uncontrollable firestorms, coastal inundation, and the melting of the polar ice caps. The warnings of a generation of scientists have been disregarded. No wonder an evolutionary anthropologist can write,

> The human story is so far without an end, but is probably heading for inevitable global catastrophe. The key question is how our denouement will come about: Will it be by nuclear devastation, man-made global warming, or biological epidemic? What a truly remarkable species we are to have provided ourselves with such options.[3]

These concerns are unfortunately nothing new. As long ago as 1968, George F. Kennan wrote presciently,

> How long can man go on overpopulating this planet, destroying its topsoils, slashing off its forests, exhausting its supplies of fresh water, tearing away at its mineral resources, consuming its oxygen with a wild proliferation of machines, making sewers of its rivers and sea, producing industrial poisons of the most dreadful sort and distributing them liberally into its atmosphere, its streams and its ocean beds, disregarding and destroying the ecology of its plant and insect life? Not much longer I suspect. I may not witness the beginning of the disaster on a serious scale. But many of the students who have written me will. And let us

not forget that much of the damage that has already been done is irreparable in terms of the insight and effort of any single generation. It takes eight hundred years to produce a climax forest. It will take more than that, presumably, to return the poisoned, deadened waters of Lake Michigan, on the shores of which I was born, to the level of plant and fish life and natural healthfulness that they had at the time of my birth.[4]

Hungering and thirsting for righteousness can be correlated with what Paul wrote about the "groaning" of the whole creation (Rom 8:22). Both are forms of intense longing. The creation, Paul taught, had been "subjected to futility" as part of the curse visited on humankind in consequence of its fall into sin (Rom 8:20; Gen 3:17–19). These groanings, the death pangs of a dying creation, were just that; but at the same time, by the grace of Christ, they were also the birth pangs leading to a glorious new world.

The themes of Romans 8:19–26 are suffering, solidarity, and hope. The earth is said to suffer from "futility" and "bondage to corruption" (Rom 8:20–21), but its groanings are not uttered alone, nor are they uttered in vain. For the faithful, or "we ourselves," wrote Paul, also "groan inwardly" in solidarity with the earth (Rom 8:23). Even more, in a kind of inconceivable *cantus firmus*, underlying the faithful in their solidarity with the earth, "the Spirit himself intercedes for us with groanings too deep for words" (Rom 8:26).

The groanings of the Spirit, the faithful, and the earth are united in a threefold communion of suffering. It is remarkable that the faithful are thought to groan precisely because they have received "the firstfruits of the Spirit" (Rom 8:23). But along with this solidarity in suffering, the Spirit also brings the promise of hope.

Romans 8:19–26 presupposes what Romans 5 and 6 teach about Christ and Adam. In particular, as set forth in those earlier chapters, Christ crucified and risen from the dead is the hidden premise of Romans 8. It is he who makes it possible for the groanings of the whole creation to be placed in a context of cosmic hope. The Christ who has made the sufferings of the world his own is the Christ who brings ultimate healing to all things. The faithful cannot remain true to Christ without remaining true to the earth.

Remaining true to the earth means participating in Christ and bearing witness to him. It means being conformed to him by caring for what he cares about, suffering with what he suffers over, and acting in analogy, if only at a distance, to his saving obedience on behalf of the world. This way of being conformed to Christ is the work of the Spirit in sanctification. As the faithful are sanctified this way, they proclaim Christ's lordship over death and attest the cosmic hope that he alone brings.

The environmental crisis of the present time can be seen as a secondary, if severe, outworking of the sufferings of creation as described by Paul. They are not the curse but an outworking of the curse, not the fall into sin but its bitter denouement. The faithful have no business condoning it, ignoring it, or collaborating with it. Their calling is to counteract it, as far as is humanly possible under the leading of the Spirit, by establishing signs of hope. Again, Kennan may be seen to point the way. As one commentator has observed,

> Whatever one's view of Kennan's stand on specific issues, his underlying philosophy contains important principles that today's policy makers ignore at our peril. These include advice to assess the facts realistically, not on the basis of some preconceived theory; to act with modesty and restraint; to keep lines of communication open; to avoid involvement in unnecessary wars; to find a means of limiting the threat to mankind posed by nuclear and other weapons of mass destruction; and to take more effective steps to preserve the planet's environment, which—in his deep if undogmatic religious faith—George Kennan believed had been bestowed upon mankind by Providence,

with the concomitant duty of acting as responsible stewards rather than despoilers.[5]

The faithful are called to act as responsible stewards, not as despoilers, in the shaping of their lives, both as individuals and as a community. Only as their lives bear the marks of responsible stewardship in loyalty and witness to Christ will they have credibility in their environmental appeals to the too-often unresponsive policymakers of this world. It could begin with something as simple as not buying nondegradable styrofoam cups, or progress to something as ambitious as adopting simpler, more sustainable lifestyles and installing solar panels in churches and at home. Nothing less would seem to be required today of those who hunger and thirst for righteousness toward an earth in crisis and perhaps terminal pain. Nothing less would seem to be required of those who know that Christ brings the world hope even where there is no hope.[6]

It is not impossible that Christians—who currently number roughly 2.2 billion persons, or roughly one-third of the world's population—may on the whole make a positive contribution to these and other efforts toward a better world. As political scientist Walter Russell Mead notes,

> The push toward democracy in many countries has been led by Christian laypeople and religious organizations. (That was not true 100 years ago; outside the English speaking world at that time many Christian churches and movements were closely tied to premodern, anti-democratic or anti-republican ideas.) From South Korea to Poland to South Africa by way of Egypt, Christians have been key players in both successful and unsuccessful democracy building movements. Will the rise of Christianity in sub-Saharan Africa promote better, more democratic government there as Christian ideas sink in more deeply among the citizens and leaders of those countries?[7]

RESILIENT COMMUNITIES

In September 2013, the highly respected Intergovernmental Panel on Climate Change (IPCC)—a United Nations agency comprised of 195 member nations who are mandated to reach unanimity—released its most recent report. Based on up-to-date scientific findings, the report concludes that most global warming since 1950 has been caused by human activities, especially the burning of fossil fuels. Droughts, wildfires, extinctions, and floods have not only begun to worsen, but are likely to persist into the foreseeable future. The signs are grim: polar icecaps are melting, sea levels are rising, and greenhouse gases are accumulating, while extreme weather events are becoming more frequent.

Meanwhile, as has been true for decades, the world's governmental leaders seem paralyzed when it comes to implementing remedies that would match the crisis. They have not adopted policies that would bring the world—especially advanced industrial societies—closer to a more sustainable way of life. The measures needed are perceived not only as being too radical but also as too threatening for powerful financial interests. Although the IPCC report states that effective measures can still be taken, some disturbing trends now seem irreversible. It has been suggested that our planet is like an overweight smoker with a heart condition. The chair of the IPCC, Dr. Rajendra Pachauri, pleads that it is now five minutes before midnight. An unsettling question can no longer be avoided. Is it reasonable to suppose that national governments will do what is needed to avert unprecedented ecological disaster?

Nongovernmental efforts are already under way to prepare for drastic, perhaps catastrophic, climate change. Some initiatives operate at the grassroots.

- Bay Localize in Oakland, California, for example, has developed a remarkable "Community Resilience Toolkit."[8]

- Bioneers, a New Mexico-based nonprofit organization, promotes local solutions to environmental challenges. It offers annual conferences, a network of community gatherings, and multimedia resources.[9]

Other organizations aim to link grassroots movements with a wider global network.

- The Transition Movement, for example, connects grassroots initiatives in the United States to similar efforts around the world. Seeking to build community resilience against fossil fuel dependency, climate change, and the economic crisis, it strives for a simpler, socially connected way of life that is abundant, fulfilling, and equitable for all.[10]

Independent high-level research groups have also been formed.

- Resilience Alliance, for example, is an interdisciplinary network of scientists and practitioners that was established in 1999. From a social-ecological systems perspective, it analyzes how people and nature are dynamically interconnected. Supported by an international network of institutions, including universities, government, and nongovernment agencies, it publishes the journal *Ecology and Society*.[11]

Worthy of special note is the Resilient Strategies organization founded by John Robb. Resilient Strategies provides individuals with information that can be put to use immediately. Comprehensive plans are offered by which a household can increase its chances of success in a difficult future by becoming resilient.[12]

Robb's resume is unusual. Starting out in the 1980s as an Air Force officer working in counterterrorism, he then switched to the field of internet technology in the '90s, finally transferring his skills more recently to developing strategies for coping with what he describes as five states of impending disaster: (1) financial collapse, (2) economic collapse, (3) political collapse, (4) social collapse, and (5) cultural collapse. Robb sees contemporary Europe, for example, as descending down the scale, Greece as having reached point four, and beyond Europe, countries like Syria and Somalia as having landed at point five. These stages he regards as an omen of the future.

As Robb envisions it, resilience is not only living sustainably or becoming independent of existing structures. It's about becoming equipped to handle acute problems—"severe storms, riots, flooding, power outages"—while also being positioned to thrive in the longer-term trends: "Financial collapse, long-term power outages or major food supply interruptions." Inefficient centralized states, as they currently exist, Robb believes, will not be able to help us, and a retreat to short-term thinking is not enough.[13] He writes,

> Our tightly interconnected global system is increasingly prone to large shocks from a variety of man-made and natural causes. These shocks can disrupt flows of energy, food, commerce, and communications to produce widespread wealth destruction (at best) and famine/death (at worst). The best way to mitigate these shocks is to build resiliency at the local level so that communities can enjoy the benefits of globalization without being damaged by its excesses. I am exploring what a community needs to do to be resilient.[14]

Robb has developed numerous detailed reports on how to create your own electricity, how to harvest very large quantities of rainwater, how to grow your own food in a limited space, how to create community-based forms of security, and much more. These strategies can be implemented by local communities as well as by individuals. Although his ideas might seem far out, they do not seem as implausible today as they would likely have seemed ten years ago. Moreover, ten years from now, if not sooner, Robb may well be so far out that he's in, especially if the concerns raised by the IPCC report are inadequately addressed. Resilient Strategies offers a ray of hope in the midst of a crisis where it otherwise seems in short supply.

Let me conclude with "17 Rules for a Sustainable Local Community" by Wendell Berry, the Kentucky novelist, essayist, and poet.[15] Berry articulates the larger vision for which Robb develops a blueprint of nuts and bolts. What Robb, Berry, and the organizations mentioned above share is an understanding that a sustainable community will look less like *The Great Gatsby* and more like *Little House on the Prairie*, if we are to avoid a nightmare future like *A Clockwork Orange*. Resilient communities, they agree, require local economies whose aim is not only generosity, but also a well-distributed and safeguarded abundance.

17 Rules for a Sustainable Local Community

by *Wendell Berry*

How can a sustainable local community (which is to say a sustainable local economy) function? I am going to suggest a set of rules that I think such a community would have to follow. I hasten to say that I do not understand these rules as predictions; I am not interested in foretelling the future. If these rules have any validity, it is because they apply now.

Supposing that the members of a local community wanted their community to cohere, to flourish, and to last, they would:

1. Always ask of any proposed change or innovation: What will this do to our community? How will this affect our common wealth?
2. Always include local nature—the land, the water, the air, the native creatures—within the membership of the community.
3. Always ask how local needs might be supplied from local sources, including the mutual help of neighbors.

4. Always supply local needs first (and only then think of exporting products—first to nearby cities, then to others).

5. Understand the ultimate unsoundness of the industrial doctrine of "labor saving" if that implies poor work, unemployment, or any kind of pollution or contamination.

6. Develop properly scaled value-adding industries for local products to ensure that the community does not become merely a colony of national or global economy.

7. Develop small-scale industries and businesses to support the local farm and/or forest economy.

8. Strive to supply as much of the community's own energy as possible.

9. Strive to increase earnings (in whatever form) within the community for as long as possible before they are paid out.

10. Make sure that money paid into the local economy circulates within the community and decreases expenditures outside the community.

11. Make the community able to invest in itself by maintaining its properties, keeping itself clean (without dirtying some other place), caring for its old people, and teaching its children.

12. See that the old and young take care of one another. The young must learn from the old, not necessarily, and not always in school. There must be no institutionalized childcare and no homes for the aged. The community knows and remembers itself by the association of old and young.

13. Account for costs now conventionally hidden or externalized. Whenever possible, these must be debited against monetary income.

14. Look into the possible uses of local currency, community-funded loan programs, systems of barter, and the like.

15. Always be aware of the economic value of neighborly acts. In our time, the costs of living are greatly increased by the loss of neighborhood, which leaves people to face their calamities alone.

16. A rural community should always be acquainted and interconnected with community-minded people in nearby towns and cities.

17. A sustainable rural economy will depend on urban consumers loyal to local products. Therefore, we are talking about an economy that will always be more cooperative than competitive.

CONCLUSION

As world Christianity comes of age, its adherents will increasingly be called to take their place among those who hunger and thirst for righteousness. They will increasingly be called to participate in Christ's sufferings in the world and to bear witness to him, by word and above all by deed, as the world's one enduring hope. They will increasingly be called to remain true to Christ by remaining true to the earth. They will find themselves entering into practical alliances with others who do not yet know Christ (or who even consciously reject him), but who are committed, along with them, to short-term goals of social justice.

Although as occasion arises they will confess their hope in Christ, they will regard all who hunger and thirst for righteousness as existing under the sign of Christ's promise. They know, as the others do not yet know, that their deepest longings for justice, peace, and the integrity of God's creation will be satisfied.

THE FAITHFUL

THE PATTERN OF INTERPRETATION FOR THE second four Beatitudes is much the same as for the first. In the second group of four, those who are said to be blessed are primarily identified as the faithful, that is, not directly as those who are needy, but as those who in allegiance to Jesus are said to be merciful, pure in heart, peacemakers, and objects of persecution for righteousness' sake. Each of these attributes is again embodied first of all in Jesus, who gives them their essential definition. Then surrounding him at the center are again the two concentric circles, consisting in an inner ring of those who know and confess him, and then of an outer ring of those who may be moved by him but as yet unawares. There is, it seems, an incognito working of grace. As Jesus himself once remarked, the children of this world in their generation are some-times wiser than the children of light (Luke 16:8).

As in the first four Beatitudes, so also in the second four: Jesus himself stands out as the promise and the blessing in one.

He alone is the source and the content of the rewards promised in the second four Beatitudes. If there are any who receive mercy, any who come to see God, any who are called God's children, and any who inherit the heavenly kingdom, then it is only in and through Jesus Christ. He himself is the unifying center of all God's promises and blessings.

5

BLESSED ARE THE MERCIFUL,
FOR THEY SHALL RECEIVE MERCY.

IN THE WORLD, THERE IS finally only one source of mercy. All merciful human deeds and inclinations—no matter what form they may take, no matter where they may be found—flow ultimately from the heart of God. God's inmost heart, as revealed in Jesus, is entirely a heart of mercy.

Mercy is the primary form that God's love for the world assumes. It is God's response to the creature's neediness and distress. In and through Jesus, God takes human misery to heart and wills effectively to remove it. No human misery or distress falls outside the mercy of God.

In Jesus the heart of God is opened and made manifest. He is the mercy of God in person on earth. He shows and imparts God's mercy in relation to our misery. He sympathizes with us in our distress and takes effective steps to remove it.

Jesus embodies the mercy of God. In his life, he had compassion on those in dire need, especially on those with no earthly hopes and no prospects for new life. Again and again, we see him acting in mercy to capacitate the incapacitated. He had compassion on the lame, the blind, the deaf, the lepers, the possessed, and even on some who were dead. In his powerful mercy and merciful power—in the sovereignty of his grace—he restored them to newness of life. He created possibilities where there were no possibilities, making a way where there was no way.

He thereby placed those whom he restored under the sign of resurrection hope. Because of him, all who languish in affliction, humiliation, and distress are included under the sign of this promise. In his death, Jesus took on their sufferings and hopelessness, entering fully into their plight. He assumes those who are afflicted into his wounded body that they might receive a share in the promise of his risen body. The mystical body of Christ includes not only the faithful but also the afflicted. The afflicted are allotted a share in his body that is wounded for their sakes.

At the same time, and supremely, Jesus brought God's mercy to the world by the forgiveness of sins. In the mercy of God, he had the power to remove our misery and, even more, the authority to deliver us from the looming judgment incurred by sin. He thereby restored us to communion with God and the hope of eternal life.

While not failing to judge our sinfulness as deplorable guilt, he nevertheless looked beyond it to the misery we suffer because of it. He knew that as we were guilty we were also enslaved by sin's disfiguring power. At untold cost to himself, he willed in his mercy to remove sin's guilt and power once for all. While we were yet helpless, he died for us (Rom 5:6). He bore our sins in his body on the tree in order that they might be destroyed (1 Pet 2:24). "He is the expiation for our sins, and not for ours only but also for the sins of the whole world" (1 John 2:2). In Jesus there is a depth of mercy sufficient to remove our afflictions and sins.

The merciful whom Jesus blesses are first of all his disciples. They are those who love and trust him in life and in death. They gladly receive the forgiveness he extends, and in the Lord's Prayer, they ask for it every day. They are thereby given a heart of flesh where they once had a heart of stone, a heart that is not callous and indifferent but merciful, a heart that cares about those in need and reaches out to them. They do the works of mercy that Jesus has prepared for them to walk in.

As they undertake these works, they are acting in and through Jesus, even as he is acting in and through them. Their appointed works are works of prayer, works of caring, and works of witness. The merciful pray for those in need, especially for the poor, the lost, the afflicted, and the oppressed, and take steps to alleviate their distress. They do so as witnesses to the mercy they have received from Jesus, and in the act of witness, they mediate his mercy, in some measure, to others, or better, he mediates his mercy through them.

It seems that the merciful whom Jesus blesses extends beyond the circle of his disciples. "For the one who is not against us is for us" (Mark 9:40). "I have other sheep that are not of this fold. I must bring them also, and they will listen to my voice" (John 10:16). Where works of mercy are performed, Jesus himself is present in the power of the Spirit, regardless of whether he is known for who he is or not yet known. To paraphrase Calvin in another connection, if we believe that the Spirit of God is the only fountain of mercy, we will neither reject nor despise the mercy itself, wherever it shall appear, unless we wish to insult the Spirit of God (cf. *Institutes of the Christian Religion* II.2.15).

It has been said that the virtues of pagans are nothing but splendid vices. Perhaps that is sometimes so, but too often the same could also be said about the "virtues" of Christian believers. Whether the genuinely merciful who do not yet know Jesus are the adherents of a particular religion or of no religion, they are nonetheless being moved by his Spirit in their mercy, and they will one day know whose Spirit it is.

Jesus is himself the promise and the blessing to all who are merciful, for he is God's mercy incarnate, and also the presence of the age to come. The merciful will receive the promise and the blessing that is offered only as they also receive him, for in this promise of mercy, the Gift and the Giver are one.

It ought not to be overlooked that the merciful are presumed by this saying to stand in need of mercy themselves. "They shall receive mercy." They are, therefore, still numbered among the needy. The merciful do not stand over against the needy but belong to them. No matter how many merciful deeds they may perform, they must still come before God with humility. At the end of all things, as well as every day along the way, one prayer must continually be on their lips: "Lord Jesus Christ, Son of God, have mercy on me, a sinner."

While it is fitting for the merciful to receive mercy as their reward, the reward is not based on their merits, except as they are gifts, for it comes to them freely from above. As cited in the *Catechism of the Catholic Church*, St. Thérèse of Lisieux strikes exactly the right note:

> After earth's exile, I hope to go and enjoy you in the fatherland, but I do not want to lay up merits in heaven. I want to work for your love alone....In the evening of this life, I shall appear before you with empty hands, for I do not ask you, Lord, to count my works. All our justice is blemished in your eyes. I wish, then, to be clothed in your own justice and to receive from your love the eternal possession of yourself. (para. 2011)

This is the prayer of the merciful for the mercy promised to them as a reward, and which comes to them freely by grace.

EXCURSUS

If the mercy of God in Jesus extends beyond the circle of his disciples, if the inner and the outer circles ultimately converge into one, then will there be any who are finally excluded? This is a difficult question, whose possible answer can only be suggested. The biblical evidence would seem to be mixed.

The letter of James is a good example. On the one hand, we read, "For judgment is without mercy to one who has shown no mercy" (Jas 2:13a). Yet immediately on its heels, we read this: "Mercy triumphs over judgment" (Jas 2:13b). The tension between these statements—judgment without mercy, on the one hand, and yet mercy triumphing over judgment, on the other— seems to run throughout Scripture as a whole.

Nevertheless, if the second statement is meant as the last word, the accent would finally fall upon it. What is clear is that there is mercy, and there is judgment. Although the one does not exist without the other, in the grace of our Lord Jesus Christ, the two will not finally conflict but will be reconciled. The merciless and despairing are judged by the mercy they refuse.[1]

Recall the parable told by Jesus about the shepherd who had lost a sheep. He left the ninety-nine in the open country, and went out searching for the one that was lost—"until he found it" (Luke 15:4). From this teaching, and others like it, we may conclude with *The Study Catechism* of the Presbyterian Church (U.S.A.),

> No one will be lost who can be saved. The limits to salvation, whatever they may be, are known only to God. Three truths above all are certain. God is a holy God who is not to be trifled with. No one will be saved except by grace alone. And no judge could possibly be more gracious than our Lord and Savior, Jesus Christ.[2]

Recall also St. Paul's words that "God has consigned all to disobedience, that he may have mercy on all" (Rom 11:32)— words which again seem at once enigmatic and yet hopeful. In

the Psalms, we read repeatedly that God's mercy "endures forever" (see esp. Ps 136). It is also written that God's anger

> is but for a moment,
>   and his favor is for a lifetime.
> Weeping may tarry for the night,
>   but joy comes with the morning.

(Ps 30:5)

These passages display notes of universal hope. The Lord
God "will swallow up death forever; and...will wipe away tears
from all faces" (Isa 25:8). Nevertheless, other well-known passages seem to run in the opposite direction.

Many distinguished recent theologians have spoken in
favor of leaving the question open in hope. Three may be briefly
noted: Kallistos Ware (Eastern Orthodox), Thomas F. Torrance
(Protestant), and Hans Urs von Balthasar (Roman Catholic).
Although none of them advocates "universalism," each draws
back from rejecting a universal hope.

Metropolitan Kallistos Ware writes,

> Hell exists as a final possibility, but several of the Fathers
> have nonetheless believed that in the end all will be rec-
> onciled to God. It is heretical to say that all must be saved,
> for this is to deny free will; but it is legitimate to hope that
> all may be saved.[3]

In a similar vein, Thomas F. Torrance suggests,

> At the very best universalism could only be concerned with
> a hope, with a possibility, and could only be expressed
> apocalyptically. But to turn it into a dogmatic statement,
> which is what the doctrine of universalism does, is to
> destroy the possibility in the necessity....True dogmatic
> procedure at this point is to suspend judgment...for here
> that is the most rational thing reason can do. Whether all

66

[human beings] will as a matter of fact be saved or not, in the nature of the case, cannot be known.[4]

Finally, we read from Hans Urs von Balthasar,

> I claim nothing more than this: that [New Testament statements speaking of hope] give us a right to have hope for all human beings....I do not wish to contradict anyone who, as a Christian, cannot be happy without denying the universality of hope....But, in return, I would like to request that one be permitted to hope that God's redemptive work for his creation might in some way prevail. Certainty cannot be attained, but hope can be justified.[5]

This much would seem to be certain: without repentance and faith, there can be no communion with God; and without communion with God, there can be no eternal life; without being moved by grace, no one can come to repentance and faith; and finally, in the inscrutable mercy of God, all persons will somehow be encountered by grace and the judgment of grace. Most certainly, God will never be another God for anyone than he has revealed himself to be in Jesus Christ. That is the only sure basis of hope. In some sense beyond all knowing, and no doubt in staggering ways, mercy will triumph over judgment.[6]

THE QUALITY OF MERCY: TWO EXAMPLES

F. KEFA SEMPANGI

F. Kefa Sempangi founded the Presbyterian Church in Uganda during the years when the dictator Idi Amin was in power. Mass murder, torture, and brutality terrorized the land. Sempangi and his congregation of nearly fourteen thousand members became targets of the regime. In 1974, he fled with his family into exile, only to return in 1979 after the dictator was deposed. Since then Sempangi has served as Deputy Minister for Rehabilitation and as a member of Parliament. In 2001, he established the Africa Foundation Children's Home, which ministers to over six thousand homeless, orphaned, and abandoned street children.

In his book *A Distant Grief*, Sempangi tells this story,

[On Easter Day in 1973 he preached to over 7,000 people, who had traveled from far and wide to attend his church. After the service, a number of Amin's Nubian assassins followed him back to the vestry and closed the door behind them. Five rifles were pointed at his face.]

"We are going to kill you for disobeying Amin's orders," said the captain. "If you have something to say, say it before you die."

I could only stare at him. For a full moment I felt the full force of his rage....

From far away I heard a voice, and I was astonished to realize that it was my own.

"I do not need to plead my own cause....I am a dead man already. My life is dead and hidden with Christ. It is your lives that are in danger, you are dead in your sins. I will pray to God that after you have killed me, He will spare you from eternal destruction."

The leader stared at Sempangi without speaking. Then he lowered his gun and said,

"Will you pray for us now?"

"Yes, I will pray for you."

"Father in heaven...you who have forgiven men in the past, forgive these men also. Do not let them perish in their sins but bring them to yourself."

It was a simple prayer, prayed in deep fear....When I lifted my head, the men standing in front of me were not the same men who had followed me into the vestry.

[From that day forward, converted by the mercy of Christ, the gunmen vowed to protect Sempangi from Amin's assassins.][7]

The Faithful

Tomás Borge (1930–2012)

Tomás Borge of Nicaragua was one of the original founders of the Sandinista National Liberation Front (FSLN) in 1961. In 1979, the FSLN overthrew the brutal dynasty and dictatorship of Anastasio Somoza, establishing a revolutionary government in its place.

In the course of the armed struggle against Somoza, Borge was captured in Managua in 1976 and severely tortured. His release, along with that of other Sandinista fighters, was secured in 1978, when the FSLN seized the National Palace. Borge's first wife, Yelba Mayorga, was not so fortunate. She was tortured, raped, and killed by the Samozan National Guard in 1979.

One day shortly after the overthrow of Somoza's regime (July 1979), Borge, the Sandinista's newly installed Minister of the Interior, was leaving his office. Orlando Costas recounts,

> A former member of Somoza's guard had been captured and was being brought to trial. Borge recognized him immediately as the man who had tortured him. Borge looked the guard straight in the eye and asked him: "Do you recognize me?" The guard answered: "No." Borge insisted: "Look at me! I was one of those you tortured! And now you will see what the Revolution will do with people like you. Shake my hand! I forgive you."[8]

In his book *Christianity and Revolution*, Borge tells the story somewhat differently.

> After having been brutally tortured as a prisoner, after having a hood placed over my head for nine months, after having been handcuffed for seven months, I remember that when we captured these torturers I told them: "The hour of my revenge has come: we will not do you even the slightest harm. You did not believe us beforehand; now you will believe us." That is our philosophy, our way of being.[9]

69

THE BEATITUDES

Borge was also a writer and poet. In a poem addressed to his former captors, he wrote,

> My personal revenge will be the right
> of your children to school and to flowers....
>
> My personal revenge will be to say to you
> "good morning" without beggars in the streets,
>
> My personal revenge will be instead of jailing you
> to lift the sorrow from your eyes....
>
> My personal revenge will be to reach to you, my brother,
> with these the very hands which
>
> Once you tore and tortured without
> being able to destroy their tenderness.[10]

CONCLUSION

The examples of Sempangi and Borge represent different aspects of mercy: the vertical and the horizontal. Through Sempangi's courageous testimony when faced with imminent death, his assailants were touched by the mercy of God (the vertical). Through Borge's astounding generosity of heart, his torturers were met with uncommon grace (the horizontal). (Most torture survivors, it should be noted, are traumatized for life. It is understandable that they can rarely think on their tormenters with good will.) We do not honor the mercy we have received from God unless we likewise extend mercy to others.

Of mercy, Shakespeare famously wrote,

> The quality of mercy is not strain'd.
> It droppeth as the gentle rain from heaven

Upon the place beneath. It is twice blest:
It blesseth him that gives, and him that takes.[11]

Shakespeare was right that mercy blesses the one who gives it as well as the one who receives it. But if mercy indeed drops like the gentle rain, it is not because it just happens. Mercy compares to the rain only in its refreshment of the earth, not in its natural causality or chance occurrence. The suggestion that it drops "from heaven" probably involves a double entendre, meaning that just as the gentle rain drops down from above, so mercy drops down from the celestial abode of God.

Indeed, Shakespeare concludes his lines on exactly that note.

It is an attribute to God himself;
And earthly power doth then show likest God's
When mercy seasons justice.

All acts of mercy must ultimately be traced back to their source in God, and therefore to Jesus as the one who uniquely embodies God's mercy. He is himself the Mercy through whom all other acts of mercy flow, whether openly as in the case of Sempangi, or more secretly as in the case of Borge. It is Jesus who has been given the authority to bless the merciful and to promise them mercy. It is he who would plead, inconceivably, from the cross, "Father, forgive them, for they know not what they do" (Luke 23:34). Without mercy there would be no hope for any of us. But with mercy there is hope for us all. Even murderers and torturers are not outside the scope of God's graceful mercy and merciful grace.

6

BLESSED ARE THE PURE IN HEART, FOR THEY SHALL SEE GOD.

THE SIXTH BEATITUDE IS notable for the way it can be interpreted in light of the sacraments. The "pure in heart" is finally a baptismal category, while "seeing God" is ultimately eucharistic. As the living center of both baptism and the eucharist, Jesus Christ is the center of this Beatitude.

Only Jesus is truly pure in heart. In one way or another, all others are disfigured by sin. In sharp contrast to the rest of humankind, we can say: Only Jesus truly loved God with all his heart, all his soul, and all his mind; and only he loved his neighbor with the same purity as he loved God and himself. Only he, without exception, never returned evil for evil, but overcame evil with good. Only he trusted in God in all his afflictions without a trace of bitterness or resentment. Only he was never duplicitous but always spoke the truth in love. Only he never used another person to his own advantage, merely as the means to an end, but always treated others—not least the lowly and the marginalized—as ends in themselves. Only he did the will of God perfectly as he was sent and commissioned to do, proclaiming the hope of God's kingdom and dying that others might live.

Only Jesus presented his whole life to God as a living sacrifice. Only he met every temptation without being overwhelmed. He was "in every respect...tempted as we are, yet without sin" (Heb 4:15). Though his heart was pure, he allowed himself to be made "impure" for our sakes. He took on the degradation of a slave and became obedient to the point of death, even death on a cross. "Therefore God has highly exalted him and bestowed on him the name that is above every name" (Phil 2:9). No one but Jesus has ever lived the sinless life of love, devotion, and gratitude that God intended for all humankind. No one but Jesus will ever be so fully human by possessing such purity of heart.

For all other human beings, being pure in heart is at best a gift and a task. It is a gift and a task in Christ and through Christ. Others can be and are pure in heart, though only as by grace they participate in him. In this life, their purity will never be more than broken and partial, but in that limited sense, purity of heart is possible, commanded, and real. It will be fulfilled and brought to perfection in us by the Holy Spirit in the life to come.

BEING MADE PURE IN HEART THROUGH BAPTISM

The disciples of Jesus receive their purity of heart from him by grace through faith. The sacramental form of this reception is baptism. Pure hearts are received as they receive him; and as they receive him, he imparts himself and his purity to them. Objectively, in Christ, they are made pure in heart before God, while subjectively, in themselves, they are not yet pure in heart, but must become so day by day.

Cleansed by the waters of baptism, they are set on the path of sanctification. This path is one of conflict between their old humanity, as still enmeshed in sin, and their new humanity, as given and received daily through work and prayer. Empowered by the Holy Spirit, they are called to become in themselves what they already are in Christ: pure in heart.

They cannot achieve purity in themselves merely by their own power. The famous prayer of St. Augustine must be on their lips: "Give what you command, and command what you give" (*Confessions* X.60). No less paradoxical description will do. While the faithful do not become pure in heart without their own efforts, even less do they do so apart from grace, on which everything depends.

Here, too, as throughout their spiritual lives, they must work as if there were no such thing as prayer, and pray as if there were no such thing as work. As stated in the summary of St. Benedict's Rule, *Ora et Labora* ("Pray and Work"). This motto applies to becoming pure in heart. Prayer for the heart's purity is inseparable from human striving, even as human striving for a pure heart is inseparable from prayer. To God alone be the glory—*soli Deo gloria*—as Bach wrote on the first page of each of his sacred cantatas, works that could never have been achieved without prayer.

Baptism is the sacrament by which the paradox of grace is best captured. While baptism is a complex topic, three elements will be singled out: baptism as the forgiveness of sins, baptism as the washing away of impurity, and baptism as being joined to Christ in his death. Purity of heart cannot be grasped apart from baptism as the washing away of impurity. Nor can the heart's purity be separated from the forgiveness of sins and union with Christ.

Baptism mediates and proclaims forgiveness to the one who is baptized. Because Christ is the hidden minister who operates through the human minister, in baptism he mediates and proclaims the forgiveness that he himself is. If we take baptism as a sacramental form of God's word, then like God's word (and in dependence upon it), baptism effects what it signifies and signifies what it effects. The word of forgiveness is fulfilled in baptism for each baptized person in particular.

In the New Testament, forgiveness is symbolized as a washing. When a person is baptized, sin is washed away "by the washing of water with the word" (Eph 5:26; cf. Acts 22:16). Baptism is a "washing of regeneration" that brings with it the "renewal of the Holy Spirit" (Titus 3:5). It cleanses the person, as it were, from head to toe.

> Purge me with hyssop, and I shall be clean;
> wash me, and I shall be whiter than snow.
>
> (Ps 51:7)

"The one who has bathed...is completely clean" (John 13:10). The baptized are cleansed in baptism from all impurity (cf. 1 John 1:9).

At the same time, through baptism they are united with Christ in his death in order to receive from him new life. Baptism is the sacramental form of dying and rising with Christ (Rom 6:4; Col 2:12). In and through the waters of baptism, the old has passed away and the new has come (2 Cor 5:17). "You have died, and your life is hidden with Christ in God" (Col 3:3).

The upshot is as follows. In principle baptized persons have been made pure in heart before God. In practice—because of the sin that still clings so closely, but whose power has been broken—they are not yet pure in heart in themselves, but must strive to become so each day. Their hope is that God, who has begun a good work in them, will not fail to bring it to completion (Phil 1:6). Purity of heart is, therefore, a promise as well as a gift and a task.

What then can be said about those in the outer ring, whose center is secretly in Christ? Do the gift, the task, and the promise of being pure in heart apply also to them? Do they apply in any sense to the unbaptized? In *Lumen Gentium*, Vatican II's "Dogmatic Constitution on the Church," this question (or one like it) is addressed. Jews, Muslims, and those of other faiths, or of no faith, are distinguished and briefly discussed (*LG* 16). A cautious openness and a bold hope are affirmed. Word and sacrament are seen as bound completely to Christ, but Christ is not bound narrowly to them. He can and does work secretly outside and beyond them, though never against or without them.

Humanly speaking, there are those *extra muros ecclesiae* (outside the walls of the church) whose purity of heart would seem to excel that of many inside the church. The faithful would do well to acknowledge them, and strive to learn from them, in so far as they can do so without contradiction to the gospel. At best, Christ can be discerned in the hearts of such outsiders from afar.

COMING TO SEE GOD THROUGH THE EUCHARIST

No one can see God who is not pure in heart. Had not the Lord intervened to wash away sins, who could stand? (Ps 130:3). The declaration "Blessed are the pure in heart" fulfills, by grace, the prior declaration of the Psalmist, "Blessed is the one whose sins are forgiven" (Ps 32:1). As sanctification flows from justification, so does the vision of God flow from sanctification. The purpose of being made pure in heart is to see God.

Seeing God is not only the soul's highest good, but also its greatest delight. Seeing God means being lost in wonder, love, and praise before the beauty of God's holiness. It means entering with thanksgiving into the gates of God's glory, and being wonderfully smitten by what one finds. The beatific vision involves, as Jonathan Edwards once suggested, having a direct and immediate sense of "the excellency and beauty of God," that is, "an immediate view of God's great and awful majesty, of his pure and beauteous holiness, of his wonderful and enduring grace and mercy."[1] The beatific vision means seeing the majesty and immensity of the God who is Father, Son, and Holy Spirit. It means seeing the full splendor of God's love for himself and all others, including oneself. To see and delight in the glory of Divine Love is the end of all things.

On the other hand, no one can see God and live (Exod 33:20). Only through some overriding form of mediation—indeed only through the grace of the Mediator—can it be possible to stand in the presence of God's holiness. "When I saw him," confessed the seer, "I fell at his feet as though dead. But he laid his right hand on me, saying, 'Fear not, I am the first and the last'" (Rev 1:17). Recall the words of Jesus in his high priestly prayer: "Father, I desire that they also, whom you have given me, may be with me where I am, to see my glory that you have given me because you loved me before the foundation of the world" (John 17:24). Seeing God cannot be separated from God's only Son, who received the divine glory from before the foundation of the world. Only through the mediation of the incarnate Son can one see God's glory and live.

Seeing God means beholding "the glory of God in the face of Jesus Christ" (2 Cor 4:6). This is an aspect of the beatific vision. It radically transforms the eye of the beholder and the being of the beholders themselves, in what the Eastern Church calls "deification." "And we all, with unveiled face, beholding the glory of the Lord, are being transformed into the same image from one degree of glory to another. For this comes from the Lord who is the Spirit" (2 Cor 3:18). To behold the glory of the Lord in the face of the risen Christ means becoming suffused, as he is, with light. "When he appears we shall be like him, because we shall see him as he is" (1 John 3:2). Seeing him as he is, the faithful are transfigured by the radiance of Divine Love.

As stressed especially by John Owen, the direct object of the beatific vision is in one sense Jesus himself.[2] At the same time, he is also the Mediator through whom the faithful are transfigured into his likeness. And as they are so transfigured, from one degree of glory to another, they are given a share, through their union with him, in his own contemplation of and delight in the Father. Jesus Christ is, therefore, the object of the beatific vision, the fountain of grace that makes it possible, and the Mediator through whom the pure in heart are transformed so as to contemplate the Father's love in heavenly glory. Through the incarnate Son, in the communion of the Holy Spirit, the faithful are blessed to behold the splendor of the Father.

The beatific vision finds its immediate occasion most fully in the eucharist. The eucharist does not so much dispense Christ to the faithful as it unites them to him, by means of his body and blood, under the forms of bread and wine. It is the highest privilege of the faithful to worship God; and in worshiping God, they discover that God's response is to give them a blessing.

The name of this blessing is Jesus Christ. It is in and through him that they come to the Father (John 14:16). "All things have been handed over to me by my Father, and no one knows the Son except the Father, and no one knows the Father except the Son and anyone to whom the Son chooses to reveal him" (Matt 11:27). The identity of Jesus is revealed most palpably in the eucharist. "He was known to them in the breaking of the bread" (Luke 24:35). The eucharistic meal as shared here and now is but a foretaste of the Great Banquet yet to come. As E. L. Mascall has written, integral to the Banquet is the beatific vision.

> They [the apostles] will be seated with their Master, who is himself the Apostle of the Father, at the messianic banquet, which, because it is the banquet of his crucified and ascended body and blood, is at the same time the perpetual liturgy wherein the Father is glorified by the eucharistic offering of him who is the Son by nature and who includes within himself all those who, because they are his members, are [children] of the Father by grace and adoption, and who in their organic unity are his mystical body and bride, the catholic church, one flesh with him. And in this perpetual liturgy, wherein the church will for ever contemplate and

adore the Father, gazing at him as it were through the eyes of Christ who is her head, everything will be transformed but nothing will be destroyed.[3]

As the One who is not only the object of the beatific vision, but also in another sense its Mediator, Jesus Christ imparts the richness of this vision in a communal setting. He imparts it, that is, in the promise of the eucharistic meal. Just as baptism takes place in the community, the beatific vision is essentially communal, not merely individualistic. As the eucharist on earth points the faithful toward the promise of the beatific vision, it also mediates it to them here and now as in a distant mirror. "For now we see in a mirror dimly, but then face to face" (1 Cor 13:12).

CONCLUSION

By joining himself to the faithful in their baptism, Jesus Christ washes away their sins and makes them pure in heart. They are henceforth called to become in themselves what they are in him. Moreover, by giving himself to the faithful in the bread and wine, and by taking them to himself, Jesus Christ is the promise and the blessing of the beatific vision, both now and forever. It is in his face, and through his eyes, that the pure in heart are blessed to see God.

BLESSED ARE THE PEACEMAKERS, FOR THEY SHALL BE CALLED CHILDREN OF GOD.

THE STATEMENT "[JESUS CHRIST] is our peace" (Eph 2:14) is one way of expressing the central message of the New Testament. In him and through him, all hostile divisions, whether vertical or horizontal—that is, whether between humankind and God or between conflicting social parties—are confessed by faith to be overcome. Although terrible conflicts obviously continue to exist, they have been rendered null and void by Christ.

In the history of the covenant, the principal social division was between Israel and the nations, whose relations were often bitter. In the mystery of Christ, however, their enmity is declared as having ended. According to Ephesians, Christ has, in his very flesh, "broken down...the dividing wall of hostility," making the ancient enemies to be one (Eph 2:14). He has created a new, unified humanity, "thereby making peace" (Eph 2:15). This peace is established "through the cross" (Eph 2:16), or more graphically, "by the blood of his cross" (Col 1:20).

The peace of Christ has a double aspect. It is already perfected on one level, while not yet fulfilled on another. It is an objective reality in the process of fulfillment. As stated boldly in the twelfth-century Easter hymn,

> The strife is o'er, the battle done;
> the victory of life is won;
> the song of triumph has begun:
> Alleluia!

The victory of life is already won against the forces of death, because Christ is risen. Inaugurated by his cross, his peace goes forth into the world. The song of triumph has begun, prevailing over every brutality that contradicts it, both now and forever. This is the faith of the church.

In Colossians 1:20, it is noteworthy that the phrase "blood of his cross" seems at once historical and eucharistic in its resonance. It pertains to both Calvary and the liturgy. If so, then the victory of the cross is made manifest in the sacrament. In the eucharist, as Christ becomes present in bread and wine, former enemies are also called to be reconciled with one another. The eucharist is the sacrament of peace.

The newfound peace between ancient enemies was created at incalculable cost. As previously suggested, it is "in [Christ's] flesh" that the "dividing wall of hostility" was broken down, and it is in his body—apparently in his crucified yet also his mystical and eucharistic body—that "one new man" is created "in place of the two" (Eph 2:14–15). In the blood of his cross (literal and eucharistic), the hostility itself has been killed (Eph 2:16).

Only as they are reconciled to God, by grace through faith, can the former adversaries be reconciled to one another (Eph 2:16). The reconciliation that results from grace transcends anything that is possible through the law—"the law of commandments expressed in ordinances" (Eph 2:15). Peace comes as a gift before it unfolds as a task.

Here are Paul's exact words:

> For he himself is our peace, who has made us both one and has broken down in his flesh the dividing wall of hostility by abolishing the law of commandments expressed in ordinances, that he might create in himself one new man in place of the two, so making peace, and might reconcile us both to God in one body through the cross, thereby killing the hostility. (Eph 2:14–16)

Christ's peace stands beyond all worldly possibilities. "Peace I leave with you; my peace I give to you. Not as the world gives do I give to you" (John 14:27). It is an all-encompassing peace with far-reaching implications. These implications are social, theological, and cosmic.

SOCIAL

The peace of Christ has wide-ranging social implications. If the wall between Jews and Gentiles crumbles to the ground, other stubborn barriers crumble with it. No demeaning social arrangement has a future. All hostile conflicts stand in contradiction to Christ, who in turn stands in contradiction to them. He is the King of kings and Lord of lords. He is the Prince of Peace. In large ways and small, he brings hostility to an end. The dark side is denied the last word. Christ's peace is operative as the divine cunning in history. What is now hidden will one day be revealed.

The basic principle was captured by Paul:

> There is neither Jew nor Greek, there is neither slave nor free, there is no male and female, for you are all one in Christ Jesus. (Gal 3:28)

Throughout history this statement has functioned like a time-release capsule. No sooner is one division dismantled to a significant degree than another emerges on the agenda. As Christ abolishes the division between Jew and Greek, so he also abolishes every unacceptable social contradiction. His cross has overthrown the domination between slave and free as well as between male and female. Whether openly or secretly, every movement for liberation has Christ at its center. He is its active source. Around Christ the one true Peacemaker, there are two concentric circles: first the church and then the world.

The faithful are called to be a vanguard of the future. In their life together, relations of dominance are openly to be named and undone (Mark 10:42). The "church militant" (*ecclesia militans*) is comprised of the faithful in history, who make up what Tertullian styled as the Christian militia, namely, those who struggle against sin, the devil, and "the rulers of the darkness of this world" (Eph 6:12). It is a struggle against "spiritual wickedness in high places" as made manifest in relationships on earth (Eph 6:12, KJV). "Take no part in the unfruitful works of darkness," the faithful are told, "but instead expose them" (Eph 5:11). In the shape of their common life, they are to embody Christ's peace on earth. Nevertheless, with honorable exceptions, the church's record on this score has often left much to be desired.

The Holy Spirit is more militant than the church. When the church does little more than reproduce the unjust and domineering social relations of the surrounding world—when it merely reinforces and legitimates them—it not only brings dishonor upon its head. It also drives the Holy Spirit outside its walls to work in more promising vineyards. Every movement for social justice that struggles to humanize a heartless world owes something to the militancy of the Holy Spirit. No matter how imperfect such a movement may be, insofar as it aims at abolishing injustice and bringing peace, it is driven by a force beyond itself. Wherever one spots "the harvest of [justice] that is sown in peace" (Jas 3:18), the Holy Spirit is sure to be at work.

In short, all efforts to eliminate social cruelty, hostile division, and crying injustice—whether inside or outside the church—flow from the peace of Christ. Whether wittingly or unwittingly, and sometimes only obliquely, these efforts objectively attest the Peace of Christ, and mediate it in some way to the world.

Every downtrodden creature who is oppressed, every woman who is abused, every child who is molested is an affront to the cross of Christ. (Not the injured party is the affront, but the ill-treatment.) The faithful, who know Christ and his peace, do well when they embody that peace in the world. Others who do not yet know what the faithful know are at times secretly moved by the Spirit in a way that puts the faithful to shame. Heaven will one day recognize them with praise.

The point, however, is this: all true peacemakers, whether inside or outside the church, are inspired by a single divine source. Since Christ is the ultimate Peacemaker, all peacemakers touched by his Spirit cannot but be numbered among the blessed.

Because the twentieth century was the bloodiest in world history, and because the new century is not off to a good start, something more must be said. The faithful are most truly the faithful when they are ready to suffer and die for peace, but never to kill for peace. They seek to right wrongs, yet never to avenge them. They strive to liberate the wretched of the earth in such a way that those responsible for their wretchedness are liberated also. They know that as followers of Christ, they are called to make peace through the instruments of nonviolence.

Whether there might be exceptions to this rule, and under what circumstances, cannot be discussed here. What matters is the basic commitment from which true peacemakers set forth.

Nonviolence was understood as basic to the gospel by Athanasius in the fourth century and by Karl Barth in the twentieth century (among many others). Christ came, Athanasius noted, for the sake of peace. He makes himself the Savior of all by uniting those once locked in hatred. When antagonists are reached by the gospel of peace, they are made new.

When they hear the teaching of Christ, they immediately
turn from war to farming, and instead of arming their hands
with swords they lift them up in prayer; and, in a word,
instead of waging war among themselves, from now on they
take up arms against the devil and the demons, subduing
them by their self-command and integrity of soul.[1]

Christ's followers refrain from retaliation. "When they are
insulted, they are patient, when robbed they make light of it, and
most amazingly, they scorn death in order to become martyrs of
Christ." They are persons who would prefer to die "rather than
deny their faith in Christ" (57). That is how they show their love
for him who "by his own love underwent all things for the world's
salvation" (90). As peacemakers, they bear witness to Christ
with their lives, their sufferings, and if necessary, their deaths.
They are called to out-think, out-live, and out-die the opposition.

Barth observed that "the whole friend-foe relationship" is
invalidated by the cross of Christ.[2] Angry denunciation, retaliation, and killing are all ruled out. So is the "fixed idea of the
necessity and beneficial value of force" (IV/2, 549). "The direction of Jesus," wrote Barth, "must have embedded itself particularly deeply in the disciples in this respect. They were neither to
use force nor to fear it" (ibid.). He noted,

What the disciples are enjoined is that they should love
their enemies (Matt. 5:44). This destroys the whole friend-
foe relationship, for when we love our enemy he ceases to
be our enemy. It thus abolishes the whole exercise of force,
which presupposes this relationship, and has no meaning
apart from it. (IV/2, 550)

The renunciation of force, Barth continued, is not an
abstract principle or inflexible rule. Nevertheless, for the faithful "there is a concrete and incontestable direction which has to
be carried out exactly as given" (ibid.). It is the direction of

"practical pacifism." "According to the sense of the New Testament," Barth concluded, "we cannot be pacifists in principle, only in practice. But we have to consider very closely whether, if we are called to discipleship, we can avoid being practical pacifists, or fail to be so" (ibid.).

SOCIAL PEACEMAKING IN ACTION

Here is what social peacemaking looks like.[3] The international "Restorative Justice" movement is a voice for creative nonviolence. With roots going back as far as the traditional practices of indigenous peoples, today this movement impinges upon an increasing number of criminal justice systems, schools, social services, and related institutions around the world. It is an approach to justice that works alongside retributive justice systems while focusing on the needs of victims, communities, and offenders. It seeks to transcend abstract laws and impersonal judicial processes designed primarily to mete out punishment.

Restorative justice seeks to hold offenders accountable, sometimes without incarceration, in a way that will satisfy victims and other stakeholders while upholding the dignity of all. Each of the affected parties takes part in finding a resolution for the wrongdoing or crime. Through "restorative circles," which involve a disciplined and often painful process of face-to-face confrontation and personal sharing—where all concerned parties are present and take part—the victims find healing, the communities can go on, and the offenders—who may come to a new level of self-understanding and remorse—agree to a form of fitting compensation. The recidivism of offenders falls sharply.

Through the restorative process, the most basic values of the participants are clarified and reinforced. The participants find that trust is restored to the community, and that while few are guilty, all are responsible (in Rabbi Abraham Heschel's memorable phrase). The community is transformed along with the victim and the offender.

Take the case of West Philadelphia High School, serving a tough inner city population. It had been on Pennsylvania's "Persistently Dangerous Schools" list for six years. Through the implementation of restorative practices and strong leadership, a huge shift took place in the culture and climate of the school. Violent and serious incidents plummeted, while rates of disciplinary procedures such as suspensions and expulsions dramatically decreased.[4]

Results like this are being reproduced in many different corners of the world. While restorative justice has enjoyed significant Christian input at every level, it is a form of peacemaking that involves theoreticians and practitioners from every conceivable background, whether it be a specific religion or none.[5]

THEOLOGICAL

The social implications of Christ's peace flow from its theological foundation. "In Christ God was reconciling the world to himself" (2 Cor 5:19). In the cross, which fulfilled his incarnation, Jesus Christ reconciled the world to God. He brought peace where there was no peace and true hope to a world where none could be found.

Jesus Christ is a unique person who came to do a unique work. In the mystery of his incarnation, he is fully human and fully divine. Being human he could share in our plight. Being divine he could overcome sin and death—as we could not. As both human and divine, he performed the work of reconciliation that was most needed but only he could accomplish. That is what makes him our peace.

Between God and the human race—between God's faithfulness and our unfaithfulness—a fatal conflict had arisen. Jesus Christ stepped into the breach. As Barth observed, "He took this conflict into his own being. He bore it in himself to the bitter end. He took part in it from both sides. He endured it from both sides."[6] Being without sin, he stood on our side as sinners, bearing the brunt of God's "No" to our sin. In the most astonishing of statements, we read, "[God] made him to be sin who knew no sin" (2 Cor 5:21). At the same time, he stood on God's side—indeed he was God—as he consented to bear the divine judgment upon us.

Our sin was condemned in his flesh (Rom 8:3). He removed the judgment by bearing it himself. He took it into his person—into his being as the incarnate Son—suffering the abandonment that would otherwise have been ours. "And at the ninth hour Jesus cried with a loud voice, 'Eloi, Eloi, lama sabachthani?' which means, 'My God, my God, why have you forsaken me?'" (Mark 15:34).

"This is what it costs God to be righteous," wrote Barth, "without annihilating us" (II/1, 399), and this is what it costs God to be merciful without annihilating his righteousness. Since righteousness is essential to God's identity as God, he could not compromise his righteousness by his mercy without destroying himself (which would be impossible). In the event of the cross, God is completely righteous and completely merciful at the same time. In Christ the divine condemnation of sin is carried out to the bitter end, even as mercy is extended to the sinner. Through a righteousness and a mercy not our own—the righteousness and mercy of God—we have received grace upon grace.

God's grace is a costly grace, God's mercy is a severe mercy, and God's love is a harsh and dreadful love. Anyone who wants only the grace, mercy, and love forgets about the agony of the cross. Anyone who sees only the cost, severity, and harshness forgets about the mercy of the incarnation and the glory of the resurrection. The divine act of negating the negation of sin cannot be had without the cross, but pure negation does not have the last word. Just as sin is essentially the negation of God, so God's "No" is the negation of sin. Nevertheless, God's "No" does not have the last word. Although there is God's "No," there is also God's "Yes." The former exists in the service of the latter, because God's "Yes" is greater than God's "No."

Therefore, "we have peace with God through our Lord Jesus Christ" (Rom 5:1). The faithful are those who receive this peace by grace through faith. Those who have not yet received it are nonetheless determined by it as something that cannot be escaped. The peace of Christ radiates out from a center that makes instruments for itself wherever it will, at times and places of its own choosing.

All peacemakers are in some sense still sinful and, therefore, fall under the judgment of grace. They fall under the *judgment* of grace, since even their best efforts cannot escape being tainted by sin. But they fall under the judgment of *grace*, since the worst consequences of their sins are held in check and overridden by a secret divine power. Always ambiguous, checkered, and fragile in this life, peacemaking points beyond itself to a larger hope.

Jesus Christ is God the Son by nature. Other peacemakers are God's children by grace. Either way, according to this Beatitude, those who make peace shall be called God's children. Because one great Peacemaker exists, there are other more modest peacemakers as well. As the Lord, he works in and through them, even as they work in and through him (regardless of whether or not this is known). The center is not without its periphery: Christ does not exist without his servants, whether in the inner or the outer circle. As the one great Peacemaker, he calls forth children of God.

Christ's presence is itself the blessing and the promise to all who strive for peace by means of peace. They do well to call upon his name (Ps 50:15). They are blessed to the degree that they participate in him and his peacemaking by grace active in love. They know that there is no way to peace, because peace is the way.

What makes them blessed? They are blessed because the risen Christ is the promise that in spite of everything their efforts are not finally in vain. Through the ages, they will have suffered many setbacks and fought the long defeat. But beyond the long defeat stands the promise of a new heaven and a new earth, where all things will be made new (Rev 21:1). On the day of resurrection, the peacemakers will be revealed in triumph as the children of God. "And night will be no more" (Rev 22:5).

COSMIC

The peace of Christ, finally, has cosmic implications. According to the witness of the New Testament, because this peace is theological, it is also cosmic as well as social. While the theological and social aspects are momentous in themselves, they are not sufficient to describe the full scope of what Christ has achieved.

As the *Pantocrator*—the Ruler of all creation—the Lord Jesus Christ must be seen as in but not of the world. It is not he who is subject to the cosmos, but the cosmos that is subject to him. As the word of God incarnate, he transcends the created order. All things came into being through him, all things are ruled by him, and all things are reconciled to God in him. He is the agent, the ruler, and the reconciler of the whole creation. As the one great Peacemaker, he comes to us not as one unknown, but as the mystery of the beyond in our midst.

These astonishing claims about Christ are made throughout the New Testament. He is described as the agent of creation:

> All things were made through him, and without him was not any thing made that was made. (John 1:3)

> Through him are all things. (1 Cor 8:6)

> For by him all things were created, in heaven and on earth. (Col 1:16)

> By him all things exist. (Heb. 2:10)

He is also described as its ruler:

> All things have been handed over to me by my Father. (Matt 11:27)

> The Father has given all things into his hands. (John 13:3)

"[Christ has] the power...to subject all things to himself.
(Phil 3:21)

All authority in heaven and on earth has been given to me.
(Matt 28:18)

Of particular interest are the passages where he is described
as reconciler and goal of all things. In Romans, it is said of Christ
that "from him and through him and to him are all things" (Rom
11:36). He is depicted not only as the source and the medium of
all things, ("from him and through him") but also as their final
goal ("to him"). In Ephesians, we read of "a [divine] plan for the
fullness of time, to unite all things in him, things in heaven and
things on earth" (Eph 1:10). Here we have the important idea of
an ultimate restoration (*anakephalaiosis*). All things are envi-
sioned as being gathered together and restored to unity in and
through Christ.

A mysterious primal disruption is said to have divided
"things on earth" from "things in heaven." For the things on
earth, the result is an appalling portion of strife, carnage, and
death. Humanly speaking, it is a disorder beyond repair.

This idea of cosmic disorder seems to be in the background
of what is perhaps the decisive New Testament statement on this
theme. In Colossians, we read,

> For in him [Christ] all the fullness of God was pleased to
> dwell, and through him to reconcile to himself all things,
> whether on earth or in heaven, making peace by the blood
> of his cross. And you, who once were alienated and hostile
> in mind, doing evil deeds, he has now reconciled in his
> body of flesh by his death. (1:19–22)

Not only is God said to have reconciled all things to himself
through Christ, whether in heaven or on earth, but this newly
minted peace is said to have been effected by the blood of the
Cross. "[God] disarmed the rulers and authorities and put them to

open shame, by triumphing over them in him" (Col 2:15). The powers are disarmed and defeated—by the foolishness of the cross.

> But God chose what is foolish in the world to shame the wise; God chose what is weak in the world to shame the strong; God chose what is low and despised in the world, even things that are not, to bring to nothing things that are, so that no human being might boast in the presence of God. (1 Cor 1:27–29)

CONCLUSION

The cross is linked with a reconciliation that is universal in scope. What Augustine once said about God can be said about reconciliation in Christ: its center is everywhere and its circumference is nowhere (Augustine, *Confessions* VI.3).

If Christ is the ever-present center surrounded by two concentric circles, those who know Christ and those who do not yet know him, then it seems that the outer circle may at last expand to somehow embrace all things. The peace of Christ knows no fundamental limits. It is destined to prevail through the weakness of the cross. And when it prevails, it will have done so, in part, through the mediation of the peacemakers it has spawned as its children.

8

BLESSED ARE THOSE WHO ARE PERSECUTED FOR RIGHTEOUSNESS' SAKE, FOR THEIRS IS THE KINGDOM OF HEAVEN.

THE LAST TWO BEATITUDES ARE concerned with persecution. Different reasons for persecution are given. Some are persecuted for righteousness' sake, while others are persecuted for
Jesus' sake. It will be assumed here that these categories, while
overlapping, are distinct.

All who are persecuted for Jesus' sake are in some sense righteous. Nevertheless, not all who are persecuted for righteousness'
sake are persecuted for adhering to Jesus. The persecution of
Christians as Christians will therefore be deferred until the next
Beatitude. Here we must ask once again about the content of
righteousness. In particular we must ask about why righteousness

is, not only something for which we hunger and thirst, but also something that can lead to persecution.

A working hypothesis will be adopted. Persons are sometimes persecuted for doing what is right, because they are seen as a threat by powerful forces. They are seen as a threat, because these forces are called into question. In the New Testament, the case of John the Baptist comes to mind. He was not persecuted for confessing Jesus. Rather, he stands as an example from Scripture of someone persecuted for righteousness' sake.

JOHN THE BAPTIST

According to the Synoptic Gospels, John the Baptist was arrested by Herod and eventually beheaded. John had denounced Herod's marriage to Herodias, who was his brother Philip's wife, at a time when Philip was still living. The marriage was in violation of Old Testament law. According to the famous story, after John had been arrested, Herodias's daughter Salome danced before Herod. The king offered her whatever she wanted in return. In consulting with her mother, she was told to ask for the head of John the Baptist on a platter. Soon thereafter the prophet was beheaded (Mark 6:14–29).

In *Antiquities of the Jews* a different story is told by Josephus, the first-century Jewish historian. According to his version, Herod feared that John and his band of followers were starting a rebellion. The king therefore ordered John to be arrested and killed (*Ant.* 18.116–18).

These stories may both be true. It is possible that Herod had more than one reason for having John arrested and eliminated. A political motive may have been combined with a more personal one.

In any case, John the Baptist ran afoul of the political authorities by posing a threat to them. The threat seems to have been both moral and political. John called into question a ruler's integrity on moral and religious grounds in a way that threatened his political legitimacy. It seems that John's charges were not without foundation. He was persecuted—and martyred—for righteousness' sake.

JESUS

Where John ran afoul of the political authorities, Jesus ran afoul of the religious authorities.[1] Where John posed a threat to political legitimacy, Jesus posed a threat to religious legitimacy. The threat posed by Jesus had two main grounds: he healed the needy on the Sabbath, and he challenged the corruption of the temple.

Jesus was condemned by the religious authorities for doing things that were "not lawful to do on the Sabbath" (Matt 12:2). His unlawful activities were concerned mainly with healing the sick. "The Sabbath was made for man," he taught, "not man for the Sabbath" (Mark 2:27). He questioned his opponents: "Is it lawful on the Sabbath to do good or to do harm, to save life or to kill?" His question was met with silence (Mark 3:4). Nevertheless, especially after the beheading of John the Baptist, Jesus could see where things were headed. According to the Gospels, he foretold more than once that he would be abused, treated shamefully, and put to death. His works of compassion on the Sabbath were an offense to religious authorities. He would undergo persecution, in part, for the sake of righteousness.

Jesus was also rejected for his protest against the temple.

> And Jesus entered the temple and drove out all who sold and bought in the temple, and he overturned the tables of the money-changers and the seats of those who sold pigeons. (Matt 21:12)

He confronted his adversaries, saying: "It is written, 'My house shall be called a house of prayer,' but you make it a den of robbers" (Matt 21:13). At his trial, charges were brought against him that he had plotted to destroy the temple. His militant opposition to temple corruption was a reason why religious authorities felt threatened by him. Like John the Baptist, Jesus too would be persecuted and put to death by powerful forces that had mounted up against him. He, too, would be treated cruelly for doing what was right, as he saw it, in the eyes of God.

THE REV. MR. SEPTIMUS HARDING

A complex example of powerful forces persecuting an innocent man can be seen in Anthony Trollope's novel, *The Warden*.[2] The case of the Rev. Mr. Septimus Harding, an elderly and kindly Anglican cleric, did not have a tragic outcome, but it is interesting in this context because Mr. Harding was both persecuted and pure in heart, while being caught in a compromising situation.

Mr. Harding had been appointed as warden of an ecclesiastical care facility, called "Hiram's Hospital," endowed in the fifteenth century to provide living quarters and a small stipend for twelve aged men. By the nineteenth century, when the story takes place, the endowment had increased significantly, but under its terms, the allotment for the men had remained fixed. On a yearly basis, the warden's income had grown to a relatively modest but still handsome £800, while that of the men remained stuck where it had always been at £80 apiece.

The warden took the needs of his men to heart, sometimes assisting them, if necessary, out of his own pocket. He conscientiously provided them with all the care and solace that he could. The men for their part did not seem unhappy with their lot.

Matters changed dramatically when a young reform-minded doctor took up the cause of rectifying the situation of the men. Mr. Harding had never given much thought to the discrepancy between their wages and his own. He had simply accepted the circumstances in which he found himself.

As a result of the reformist efforts, Mr. Harding was subjected to a campaign of public humiliation. A daily London newspaper, *The Jupiter*, excoriated him harshly through an extended series of editorials. Ranking clerics, on the other hand, privately defended him and his privileges. The warden found himself in a moral quandary.

Septimus Harding was a moral man in an immoral society, if ever there were one. He was enmeshed in unjust circumstances, while still being pure in heart. The vilification to which he was subjected was arguably greater than the injustice, such as it was, of his position as the warden. He suffered persecution in having his reputation smeared by the press.

The good Mr. Harding was moved by more than a concern about his reputation. "He was not so anxious to prove himself right, as to be so" (36). He would prefer to beg in the streets than to "live in comfort on money which is truly the property of the poor" (236). Sufficient doubts arose in his heart that he at last resigned from his post. He took a large cut in pay and served out his days as the rector of a small village parish. He did so happily and without bitterness.

As far as he could, Mr. Harding tried to make all things work together for the good. Although he was not persecuted for being righteous, he was a righteous man who was persecuted. He therefore represents a limit case for the Beatitude. He helps us to see that the spirit of the Beatitude is opposed to persecution period, not just when directed against those who stand for righteousness. Persecution for any reason is a grievous wrong, and doubly so when suffered for righteousness' sake.

GANDHI AND THE SALT MARCH

In India, the movement for independence from British colonial rule, under the leadership of Mohandas Gandhi, offers numerous examples of nonviolent protestors being persecuted for righteousness' sake. In the famous Salt March of 1930, the persecution took the form of police brutality. The protest was not only against the British monopoly on the collection and manufacture of salt, but also against the related salt tax. Although common people who lived near the sea could evaporate the water and obtain their own salt, to do so and to sell it was a criminal offense. Gandhi chose salt as a focus of protest against the indignities of British rule, which he once described as a curse.

In March 1930, Gandhi staged a long march to the Indian Ocean with a huge throng of followers. When he arrived at the sea, he picked up a few pieces of salt to begin the action. Eventually, over fifty thousand Indians were imprisoned for breaking the salt laws. Their protest was carried out with disciplined nonviolence.

A report by the English journalist Webb Miller did much to expose the colonialist brutality of the British to the outside world. In a vivid eyewitness account, the journalist wrote,

> Gandhi's men advanced in complete silence before stopping about one-hundred meters before the cordon. A selected team broke away from the main group, waded through the ditch and neared the barbed-wire fence....
>
> Receiving the signal, a large group of local police officers suddenly moved towards the advancing protestors and subjected them to a hail of blows to the head delivered from steel-covered Lathis (truncheons). None of the protesters raised so much as an arm to protect themselves against the barrage of blows. They fell to the ground like pins in a bowling alley. From where I was standing I could hear the nauseating sound of truncheons impacting against unprotected skulls. The waiting main group moaned and drew breath sharply at each blow. Those being subjected to the onslaught fell to the ground quickly writhing unconsciously or with broken shoulders....
>
> The main group, which had been spared until now, began to march in a quiet and determined way forwards and were met with the same fate. They advanced in a uniform manner with heads raised—without encouragement through music or battle cries and without being given the opportunity to

avoid serious injury or even death. The police attacked repeatedly and the second group were also beaten to the ground. There was no fight, no violence; the marchers simply advanced until they themselves were knocked down.[3]

Webb Miller later visited a hospital, where he counted 320 men injured and two dead.

The Salt March was a turning point in India's struggle for independence. It galvanized the people in a way that caused actions of mass nonviolent civil disobedience to spread. Although independence would not come for many years, the Salt March was decisive in exposing the illegitimacy of British rule.

India's protestors, who prayed, marched, and sacrificed, who suffered unjust imprisonment and brutal beatings—sometimes at the cost of their lives—can be said to have been persecuted for righteousness' sake. Decades later they would inspire struggles against racial segregation and oppression in the American Civil Rights Movement, in the movement against apartheid in South Africa, and in other nonviolent movements against injustice around the world.[4]

CONCLUSION

All these persons and groups can be seen as standing under the sign of blessing as pronounced by this Beatitude. On the whole, they were persecuted for resisting injustice by nonviolent means. They took a courageous stand for righteousness and paid a heavy price.

People like this belong in one or another of the two concentric circles surrounding Jesus. Some were his committed disciples, others had a different self-understanding. The promise made to them is that theirs is the kingdom of heaven, the same promise issued in the first Beatitude to the poor in spirit. For the Beatitudes, the persecuted and the poor in spirit are in some sense one.

The promise of the kingdom belongs to them not because of their "works righteousness," but because they were moved by a hidden grace, whether they were aware of it or not. That same grace will one day reveal to them the hidden source by which their righteous actions, insofar as they were righteous, were moved. Whether they belong to the inner or the outer circle, the veil will one day be lifted, and the promise fulfilled:

> So that at the name of Jesus
> every knee should bow,
> in heaven and on earth and under the earth,
> and every tongue confess
> that Jesus Christ is Lord,
> to the glory of God the Father.
>
> (Phil 2:10–11)

The knees of all—especially the knees of those who hungered and thirsted for righteousness, of those who strove for peace, and of those who were persecuted for righteousness' sake—will bow. It will be revealed to them at last that in the midst of their earthly aspirations, struggles, and persecutions, they were not alone. They will see and acknowledge the Crucified Lord who was with them all along. They will know that by his resurrection he has prevailed. And he will give them what he has always given. He will give them simply himself, and with himself the kingdom of heaven.

THE FINAL WORD

BLESSED ARE YOU WHEN OTHERS REVILE YOU AND PERSECUTE YOU AND UTTER ALL KINDS OF EVIL AGAINST YOU FALSELY ON MY ACCOUNT.

REJOICE AND BE GLAD, FOR YOUR REWARD IS GREAT IN HEAVEN, FOR SO THEY PERSECUTED THE PROPHETS WHO WERE BEFORE YOU.

THE NINTH BEATITUDE FORMS an unexpected climax to the whole. It is noteworthy for the way that it connects persecution with adhering to Jesus, and also for the way that it combines the needy and the faithful into one. Being reviled and persecuted because of Jesus enrolls the faithful into the ranks of the needy, even as Jesus in his faithfulness became needy for our sakes. In this sense there is no longer a distinction in practice between faithfulness and neediness, for the two converge into one. At the same time, the blessing and the promise of Jesus receive perhaps their deepest expression of hope.

This particular Beatitude needs to be seen, first of all, in relation to another one from outside the Sermon on the Mount: "Blessed is the one who is not offended at me" (Matt 11:6).

Throughout his ministry, Jesus was a cause for offense. He became offensive not only to his enemies but also to his disciples. As Barth points out, "All the contemporaries of Jesus, including his most intimate disciples, finally took offense at him."[1] To his disciples, taking offense meant seeking refuge in denial or flight. To his enemies, it meant resorting to persecution.

Jesus was persecuted and condemned mainly because he was seen as committing blasphemy. Matthew offers a vivid account of what took place at his trial:

> Then the high priest tore his robes and said, "He has uttered blasphemy. What further witnesses do we need? You have now heard his blasphemy." (Matt 26:65)

To tear one's robes was a dramatic way of signifying grief and distress. Blasphemy meant claiming a status that belongs only to God. All four Gospels portray Jesus as someone who acted and spoke as though he were God, and they all depict blasphemy as central to the charges pressed against him (although in Luke, this is only implicit).

Because of the radical claims he made about his identity, both implicitly and explicitly, Jesus was an offense to the religious authorities. When the faithful were later persecuted and martyred for confessing him as Lord, they were only following in his train. The prophets who were persecuted and killed before him, as mentioned in the Beatitude, in effect prefigured the cross, while the faithful who were persecuted after him bore witness to it.[2]

Jesus seemed to make himself equal with God, not only by

what he said about himself, but also by what he did. An example of "blasphemy by deed" can be found in Mark's Gospel. In the eyes of the religious authorities, Jesus caused a scandal by forgiving a man's sins. According to Mark, when some of the scribes saw him do this, they said to themselves, "Why does this man speak like that? He is blaspheming! Who can forgive sins but God alone?" (Mark 2:7). By placing this story at the beginning of his Gospel, Mark poses the most fundamental question about Jesus. Was he guilty of blasphemy, or did divine authority really belong to him?

An example of "blasphemy by word" can be taken from Matthew's Gospel.

> All things have been handed over to me by my Father, and no one knows the Son except the Father, and no one knows the Father except the Son and anyone to whom the Son chooses to reveal him. (Matt 11:27)

Here Jesus is depicted as the divine Son. He asserts a unique and exclusive divine authority. His dominion is unique, his knowledge of the Father is unique, and his mission in making God known is unique. As the Son, he claims the status of being in communion with God the Father as an equal.

Much the same set of claims runs throughout the Gospel of John. For example:

> I and the Father are one. (John 10:30)

> No one comes to the Father except through me. (John 14:6)

While making the same picture even sharper on these points, the Gospel of John is in essential agreement with the other Gospels.

> This was why the Jews were seeking all the more to kill him, because not only was he breaking the Sabbath, but he

105

was even calling God his own Father, making himself equal with God. (John 5:18)

As depicted in all four Gospels, Jesus did many things to cause offense. He broke the Sabbath, he held suspicious views about the Law, he mixed with tax collectors and sinners, he foretold the destruction of the temple, and he denounced the religious authorities as hypocrites. As the Son of Man who would come to judge the world, he also claimed, in effect, to be their future Judge. Above all, he forgave sins, he claimed a unique communion with God as his Father, and he behaved in such a way as to be accused of blasphemy. It was primarily for this offense that he was despised, rejected, and eventually condemned to death.

EXCURSUS

Of course modern biblical scholars have sometimes doubted the historical accuracy of this picture. They have been skeptical that it corresponds to what Jesus actually did and claimed about himself. Many complicated questions are at stake that cannot be tackled here. One observation will have to suffice.

The faith of the church rests on the apostolic testimony as contained in Holy Scripture. It accepts this testimony as reliable in all essentials, unless truly compelling reasons arise not to do so. No such reasons actually exist. Although plausible pictures can be constructed that are contrary to the faith of the church, there are distinguished New Testament scholars whose work supports it. They uphold the picture of Jesus as someone who was condemned to death for blasphemy because of the highly offensive claims that he made, whether directly or indirectly, about himself.

The church's faith does not rest only on historical evidence, but primarily on the work of the Holy Spirit through the proclamation of the word of God. "Faith comes from hearing, and hearing through the word of Christ" (Rom 10:17). Faith does not necessarily need to be confirmed by modern criticism. At a minimum, it simply needs not to be disconfirmed. Despite overconfident claims to the contrary, it can safely be said that after three hundred years of modern criticism, this kind of disconfirmation has not emerged for anything essential. The accuracy of the picture of Jesus as presented here is at least as well attested as other, more skeptical views, if not more so.[3]

JESUS AS OFFENSE

Søren Kierkegaard reflected at length on the theme of Jesus as a cause for offense. He wrote, "The possibility of offense is the crossroad, or it is like standing at the crossroad. From the possibility of offense, one turns either to offense or to faith, but one never comes to faith except from the possibility of offense."[4] Two main factors, he argued, must give cause for offense: (1) the scandal of particularity, and (2) the scandal of the cross. The first involves the scandal that a mere human being could make himself equal with God, while the second focuses on the belief that God appeared under the form of his opposite in a mangled human body hanging from the cross.

The scandal of particularity was, in effect, the main reason why Jesus was persecuted at the hands of the religious authorities, while the scandal of the cross was effectively the reason why his (male) disciples at first panicked and fled. Down through the ages, those who have not fled but remained loyal to Jesus have found that they too are in danger of being persecuted or even killed for their convictions:

> A disciple is not above his teacher, nor a servant above his master. (Matt 10:24)

> "A servant is not greater than his master." If they persecuted me, they will also persecute you. (John 15:20)

All who desire to live a godly life in Christ Jesus will be persecuted. (2 Tim 3:12)

THE PERSECUTION OF CHRISTIANS

Despite being associated largely with the early church, martyrdom and persecution have rarely been absent from church history, while in the twentieth century the statistics exploded. By the year 2000—and this is a staggering figure—nearly seventy million Christians had been killed for their faith, with 65 percent of them dying in the twentieth century alone.[5] Then, as the twenty-first century unfolded, an estimated 270 new Christian martyrs were produced every day, for a total of one million within the first decade.

Martyrdoms today continue to mount. In 1900, the average number of Christian martyrs per year was less than thirty-five thousand. The projected figure for 2025 is 210,000 per year.[6]

Persecution and martyrdom are matters of degree. Martyrdoms can vary in magnitude and intensity, with "magnitude" referring to sheer numbers, and "intensity" to the number of martyrs relative to the population of Christians in a given locale. Persecution itself can assume many different forms. It ranges from the terror induced by martyrdom situations, which often involve torture and imprisonment, down to nonmartyrdom situations, with abuses like discrimination, suppression, beatings, prejudice, and ridicule.

In the early church, organized persecution was comparatively rare until the mid-third century. Nevertheless, Christians did not live in a friendly environment. Mob violence at the local level could break out at any time. Christians were perceived not only as atheists, cannibals, and incest perpetrators, but also as threats to national security. The traumas of the apostolic era (30–75 CE) left a lasting impression on the church.

Two of these traumas may be singled out for comment. First, there was the imperial persecution provoked by Nero in 64.

Although confined to the city of Rome, it produced an estimated five thousand Christian martyrs, including, according to tradition, the apostles Peter and Paul.[7] Tacitus described what took place:

> Mockery of all sorts was added to their [Christians'] deaths. Covered with the skins of beasts, they were torn by dogs and perished, or were nailed to crosses, or were doomed to the flames and burnt, to serve as a nightly illumination, when daylight had expired. (*Annals* XV.44)

An indelible mark was seared into the church's memory. Nero also outlawed Christianity as an "illegal religion," a situation that would persist, with occasional letups, until Constantine in 324.

Not long afterwards, the Great Revolt against Rome took place in Judea (66–73). In retaliation, Jerusalem was besieged and the temple demolished. Jewish Christianity was destroyed along with them. An estimated ten thousand Christians, among others, were killed.

From 70 to 249, the Eastern churches, though often neglected in modern Western histories, suffered tens of thousands of martyrdoms (cumulatively) in places like Antioch, Armenia, Cyprus, Libya, Jerusalem, and Egypt. The later empire-wide persecutions by Decius (249), Valerian (277), and Diocletian (303), though unevenly enforced, produced martyrs numbering in the hundreds of thousands.

Various features of martyrdom emerged in the early period (33–500) that would be important for the future.

- First, persecuted Christians tended to fall into three groups: the "fanatical," who openly sought martyrdom; the "realists," who capitulated in order to avoid suffering; and the "steadfast," who preferred to die, if necessary, rather than renounce their faith in Christ. The proportions of these groups would vary with time and circumstance, but in the long run, it was the steadfast that made a difference.

- Second, when possible, flight, hiding, or dispersion was an honorable solution that tended to spread the gospel to new regions and peoples. The first instance occurred after the martyrdom of Stephen (ca. 34–35), when Jerusalem Christians scattered "throughout the regions of Judea and Samaria" (Acts 8:1).
- Third, the powerful example of the martyrs—their unshakable conviction, their astonishing courage, and their refusal to retaliate—often served to win others to Christ. Leaders like Justin Martyr and perhaps Tertullian, who became Christians after witnessing brutal martyrdoms, would be examples from the early church.
- Finally, the gates of hell did not prevail against them. Despite many bleak periods of apparent hopelessness, persecutions would somehow cease, hostile rulers would die unexpectedly, circumstances would take a surprising turn for the better, violent suppression of the church in one area would be counterbalanced by its flourishing in another, and so on. For example, despite "what may have been the harshest and most widespread persecution of the church in all history," the church in China today numbers at least eighty million believers, with perhaps as many as 130 million.[8] Two thousand years of persecution would take heavy toll, but did not succeed.

A BRIEF THEOLOGY OF PERSECUTION

The ninth Beatitude promises that the faithful will be blessed when they are persecuted falsely on Jesus' account. It is a promise pertaining to this life and the next. It gains particular force because Jesus himself is always secretly the object of persecution whenever others are persecuted in his name.

The voice heard on the road to Damascus—"Saul, Saul,

why are you persecuting me?" (Acts 9:4)—indicates that when Christians are persecuted, Jesus is being persecuted along with them. "I am Jesus, whom you are persecuting" (Acts 9:5). Between Jesus and his followers, a bond exists that can never be broken, not even by persecution. He is present to them in their sufferings, and they are present to him. His presence is at once the promise and the blessing. In him the steadfast are "persecuted, but not forsaken; struck down, but not destroyed" (2 Cor 4:9).

"Participation" is a better category for understanding this mystery than "completion." The church does not, and could not possibly, "complete" the sufferings of Christ. It is not as though his sufferings were somehow deficient or in need of being supplemented. They belong to his saving perfection. There is nothing imperfect about either his person or his work. "In him the whole fullness of deity dwells bodily" (Col 2:9).

Nevertheless, as Christ has suffered once in his person, so he suffers daily in his members. The sufferings of the church are in some sense the sufferings of Christ, because the church is his body and he is its head. The faithful suffer in and through him, and he suffers in and through them. He lives in the perfect fulfillment that will one day be theirs and that belongs to them even now. Yet he does not forsake them in their sufferings but takes their sufferings to himself.

> This sharing is a two-way sharing. We share in his sufferings, and he shares in ours....To share Christ's shame is a glorious privilege, to have his fellowship—though it be in the midst of the flames—is to have fullness of joy, and to partake of his humiliation in this world is the pledge of participation in his glory in the world to come.[9]

"Correspondence" is a category that belongs with "participation." The sufferings of the church *correspond* to the sufferings of Christ. In this correspondence, they bear witness to him in his saving significance. He alone is the Lord, and they are his servants. He alone is the Savior, and they are his witnesses. The Lord bears witness to himself through their sufferings, and their sufferings bear witness to him.

The sufferings of the persecuted church are, therefore, not the same as the sufferings of Christ. They follow him at a distance. His sufferings were unique and unrepeatable. They took place once for all to redeem the whole world. Their sufferings are on a very different level as they enter into conformity with his.

Their sufferings have the function of bearing witness, while his brought about expiation and atonement. He alone is "the Lamb of God" who bears the world's sin and bears it away (John 1:29)—including that of his persecuted disciples. Their sufferings express their concrete fellowship with him. They are assigned a prophetic role. They attest, but do not contribute to, his work of reconciling of the world to God (2 Cor 5:19). For that reconciling work is finished and unrepeatable, having taken place once for all.

In the New Testament, the faithful are constantly encouraged to rejoice as they "share Christ's sufferings" (1 Pet 4:13). To "share abundantly" in his sufferings (2 Cor 1:5) means to share abundantly in his glory and joy. "For I consider that the sufferings of this present time are not worth comparing with the glory that is to be revealed to us" (Rom 8:18).

This is the promise of the Beatitude that comes to the persecuted. They may rejoice and be glad, for great is their reward in heaven (Matt 5:9). When Christ who is their life appears, they will appear with him in glory (Col 3:4). It is a promise that the cross of present reality cannot abolish resurrection hope. The sufferings of the faithful in persecution are transcended by a higher joy.

In conclusion, Jesus is the hidden center of the ninth Beatitude, just as he is the center of all the rest. When the faithful are humiliated, beaten, tortured, and killed, through love and obedience to him, he himself is the secret target of the persecution. His presence to the faithful in persecution is at once the blessing and the promise. It is the blessing that they are not alone in their suffering, and the promise that it is not in vain. Christ

within them is the hope of glory, in this life and the life to come
(Col. 1:27).

> Christ be with me, Christ within me,
> Christ behind me, Christ before me,
> Christ beside me, Christ to win me,
> Christ to comfort and restore me.
> Christ beneath me, Christ above me,
> Christ in quiet, Christ in danger,
> Christ in hearts of all that love me,
> Christ in mouth of friend and stranger.[10]

PERSECUTION BY CHRISTIANS

We could end at this point were it not for one of the most
shameful aspects of church history. Christians have not only
been persecuted in conformity to Christ. They have also become
persecutors in disgrace to Christ. The church's resort to persecution is an outrage almost without parallel in its history. It compares, if at all, only to such unthinkable developments as the
sexual abuse of children by priests. A church that resorts to persecution comes close to transforming itself into the antichrist of
its most nightmarish fears.

The targets of Christian persecution throughout history
make for a dizzying list. They include Jews, pagans, Muslims,
witches, scientists, gays and lesbians, heretics, and, not least, fel-
low Christians (and even this is not the whole catalogue). Only
brief notice can be paid to this tragedy, with no attempt to be
exonerating or exhaustive.

The church's treatment of Jews most probably eclipses all
other contradictions in its history. No sooner had Constantine
terminated the Diocletian persecution than he curtailed the
rights of Jews with the Edict of Milan (313), otherwise celebrated for its religious toleration. That was essentially the beginning of a long, dark march through the centuries in which Jews

113

were ostracized, persecuted, tortured, forcibly converted, exiled, and massacred at the hands of Christians.

After the Shoah, the Nazi holocaust in the mid-twentieth century, the churches began belatedly to rethink the monstrous idea that the Jews as a people were responsible for crucifying Christ. How this error could ever have arisen is almost inconceivable. As rightly acknowledged by the lenten hymn:

> Who was the guilty? Who brought this upon thee?
> Alas, my treason, Jesus, hath undone thee!
> 'Twas I, Lord Jesus, I it was denied thee;
> I crucified thee.[11]

The proper conclusion, which the church has yet fully to assimilate, was drawn by Hans Küng:

> Nazi anti-Judaism was the work of godless, anti-Christian criminals. But it would not have been possible without the almost two thousand years' pre-history of "Christian" anti-Judaism. None of the anti-Jewish measures of the Nazis—distinctive clothing, exclusion from professions,…forbidding of mixed marriages, expulsions, the concentration camps, massacres, gruesome funeral pyres—was new. All that already existed in the so-called Christian Middle Ages…and in the period of the "Christian" Reformation. What was new was the racial grounding of these measures.[12]

It is hard to see why the Apostle's words would not apply to the church in its anti-Judaism as well as in all its other resorts to persecution: "You are severed from Christ,…you have fallen away from grace" (Gal 5:4). In making itself guilty of Jewish blood, it is hard to see why, from a Christian point of view, the church has not thereby made itself "guilty concerning the body and blood of the Lord" (1 Cor 11:27).

According to Holy Scripture, the Jews are the people of God and the heirs of an eternal covenant (e.g., Isa 54:10).

Though they have not embraced Jesus Christ, they have not been disavowed by him (Rom 11:1). The future of God's promise belongs also to them (Rom 11:26).

From a Christian point of view, as suggested in this essay, whenever God's people are abused, there is always a secret companion who remains one with them: Jesus the Jew. He cannot be severed from his people, the Jews. It would seem that here again the voice heard on the road to Damascus cannot be entirely irrelevant. "I am Jesus whom you are persecuting" (Acts 9:5).

The conclusion seems clear. When Jews are persecuted, Jesus is persecuted along with them. That is why Karl Barth could write that "anti-Semitism is the sin against the Holy Ghost."[13] Anti-Semitism is not only a world-historical crime; it is also a form of blasphemy that approaches the unforgivable.

Nothing has done more to discredit Christianity in the eyes of the world than the church's resort to persecution, regardless of the target. Beyond the case of the Jews, as already suggested, other blood has stained the church's hands as well, from Constantine to the present. Nor should it go unmentioned that the persecution of Christians by Christians has brought special shame upon the church.

Resorting to persecution contradicts the church's holy nature as well as its essential mission. It is an intrinsic evil that can never be justified. It can only be acknowledged with sorrow, grief, and repentance: Never again!

The crucified Jesus stands at the center of a very large magnitude that includes all who are persecuted and martyred, Christian and non-Christian alike. They may or may not be conscious of him, but he is conscious of them. His relation to them is not undifferentiated, but forms a complex unity.

The faithful who are reviled, persecuted, and martyred on his account stand in the most intimate relation to him. They are the ones mentioned in the ninth Beatitude. They are the ones to whom the promise and the blessing of Jesus most immediately belong. They are, however, sadly accompanied by many others. Again, we encounter two concentric circles around a single center.

Unlike the persecuted faithful, the others do not yet know of their ultimate hope. They do not yet know that they too are within the orbit of an infinite compassion grounded in the mystery of Christ. They do not yet know of the great day that is drawing nigh. They do not yet know that because he lives they will live also, and that they too, along with many others, are placed under the sign of an invincible hope.

REMEMBRANCE

The proper response to persecution and martyrdom can be summed up by the word *remembrance*. The church has a special responsibility to remember the martyrs it has suffered, the martyrs it has killed, and, not least, those being persecuted and martyred today. Remembrance, with all that it includes, is the church's chief way of showing solidarity with each group.

Remembrance finds its proper setting in eucharistic worship and in the actions that flow from it. In and through eucharistic worship, persecution can be resisted and endured, hope can be renewed, and steps can be taken toward responsible assistance.[14] Remembrance in eucharistic worship is how the church commends the persecuted and the martyred to God, who holds the destiny of us all in his hands. It is also what empowers the faithful to act in accord with what they fervently pray.[15]

It is not a good sign when large sectors of the church fail to undertake this remembrance. It suggests the existence of out-of-touch Christians who are more spiritually obtuse than devout. It would seem that the stakes are high. Failure to remember the persecuted and the martyred—those the church has suffered and those the church has perpetrated—can only evoke the wrath of God (Rom 1:18). "But because of your hard and impenitent heart you are storing up wrath for yourself on the day of wrath when God's righteous judgment will be revealed" (Rom 2:5).

It is to the credit of recent popes that once again "remembrance" has begun to receive its due. Under the direction of Pope John Paul II, plans for a new martyrology were launched that would compile a list of twentieth-century martyrs. In a bold ecumenical gesture, the list was scheduled to include not only Roman Catholic martyrs but also Orthodox, Anglican, and Protestant martyrs. The pope wonderfully referred to this comprehensive acknowledgment as the "ecumenism of the saints." Such a *"communio sanctorum,"* he stated, "speaks louder than the things which divide us."[16]

With honorable exceptions, many Anglican and Protestant Churches have yet to rise to the impressive standard set by John Paul II and continued under Benedict XVI. Nevertheless, not even this level of remembrance is finally enough. Because in terrible ways the "communion of saints" (*communio sanctorum*) has too often been the "communion of sinners" (*communio peccatorum*), the ecumenism of the martyrs needs to be widened still further by way of formal liturgical recognition. The *communio sanctorum* needs to remember with penitence and contrite hearts the martyrs it has killed and not only those it has produced.

It should not be forgotten, for example, that in the United States, many white Christians were involved in the lynching of blacks and that these lynchings were not publicly condemned but tacitly condoned by supposedly mainstream churches. More precisely, since most blacks in these situations were believers, it is they who belonged to the persecuted church (although they were persecuted for being black and not directly for their faith in Christ).[17] Between 1882 and 1968, but mostly from 1882 to 1920, nearly 3,500 African Americans were lynched in the United States.[18]

Today an estimated 75 percent of all religious persecutions in the world are directed at the church. The Christians caught up in them—who often suffer at the hands of religious extremists of other faiths—must not be forgotten.[19] Their remembrance is essential, as is the remembrance of those of other faiths (or of no faith) who have been persecuted by professing Christians.

117

The church would only gain in credibility and integrity if it did more to institute the remembrance of those it once persecuted in liturgy and prayer. It might even inspire, in unexpected ways, greater aid to the persecuted churches today. The reward promised to the persecuted in heaven needs to find its fitting counterpart on earth.

"Do this in remembrance of me" (Luke 22:19; 1 Cor 11:24). In the ancient church, the martyrs were regularly remembered in the context of eucharistic worship, and in some communions this practice continues today. The broken bodies of the martyrs are remembered with the broken body of Christ. Those slain for the word of God are said, in the vision of the seer, to have a place under the heavenly altar, where they are clothed in robes of white (Rev 6:10–11). The place of their heavenly memorial is the eternal eucharist.

The Crucified Lord does not exist without the faithful in heaven and on earth, and most especially not without those who have paid the ultimate price. Together they constitute the mystical body of which he himself is the head. It is not fitting to remember him in the eucharist on earth without remembering those in heaven who died for his sake.

CONCLUSION

IN THIS WORK THE BEATITUDES have been presented as the self-interpretation of Jesus. Jesus is the one who defines in his person the meaning of each Beatitude. By his life, but most of all by his passion and death, he has made himself one with the needy. He himself is the defining instance of what it means to be poor in spirit, what it means to mourn, what it means to be meek, and what it means to hunger and thirst for righteousness. He entered into complete solidarity with all those who bear these privations.

At the same time, his solidarity is tempered by his singularity. His oneness with the needy places a special limit on their oneness with him. He alone was sent to remedy their neediness from within. He alone was equipped to do for the needy what none of them could do for themselves, whether individually or collectively. He was needy in their place and for their sakes, before God, so that in and through him their neediness might be remedied once and for all.

By the same token, he made himself one with all the faithful, or better, all the faithful are what they are only in and through him (whether openly or, for the time being, secretly). Again, by his life, but supremely by his passion and death, he himself defines what it means to be merciful, what it means to be pure in heart, what it means to be a peacemaker, and what it means to be persecuted for righteousness' sake. Likewise, his singularity means that he is not only the ultimate source of these virtues for all others, but also that he fulfilled them in a unique and unrepeatable way.

No one else will ever be merciful in the way that he was merciful, for he himself is the very mercy of God for our sakes, first on earth but now also in heaven. No one else will ever be pure in heart as he was pure in heart, for he himself has sanctified our humanity in his flesh in order that in and through him we might be made fit for communion with God. No one else will ever be a peacemaker as he was a peacemaker, for he himself is our Peace, who died to put an end to death, and therefore to all the things that make for death, including warfare, humiliation, persecution, enmity, idolatry, and abuse. Finally, no one else will ever be persecuted as he was persecuted, for he was maltreated, not only because of the righteousness he embodied, but also because of his singularity, namely, the offense of his exclusive oneness with God.

As suggested by the Beatitudes, his very presence to the needy and the faithful is at once a blessing and a promise. He himself is the blessing he pronounces, even as he himself is the promise he extends. He is the blessing, because his presence means that the needy are not forgotten by God. He is also the promise, because his presence means that sin, evil, and death do not have the last word. Jesus stands as the guarantee that there is an abyss of love deeper than the abyss of our despair.

The Beatitudes are often taken as moral imperatives. While that is not wrong, they are indicatives before they are imperatives, and they are imperatives only because they are first indicatives. The Beatitudes are stated in the indicative mood. They make factual statements before they express commands. They state astonishing things about the needy and the faithful as seen by the eyes of God. At heart, moreover, the Beatitudes are always secretly statements about Jesus, in his neediness and faithfulness on our behalf. His self-giving is the indicative that establishes the duty of the faithful. As his witnesses, they are called to go and do likewise. They are to give themselves for others as he has given himself, and continues to give himself, for them—and for the sake of the world.

The Beatitudes are also stated in the passive voice. The phrases "blessed are..." and "for they shall be comforted (or called, etc.)..." are divine passives.[1] The divine passive occurs when an action is ascribed to an unnamed agent, and that agent is understood to be God. Only God can be the source of the blessings and promises of the Beatitudes, and only Jesus has the divine authority on earth to utter them in the indicative mood. He not only expresses these indicatives, but also embodies and guarantees them.

Along with these indicatives, certain imperatives are clearly implied; that is, certain actions are invited and required as a fitting response to the Beatitudes' blessings and promises. However, the imperatives too should be viewed christologically first, and only then as pertaining to others. Insofar as the personal attributes (being meek, being merciful, and so forth) imply ethical imperatives, Jesus has already embodied and fulfilled them on our behalf. Insofar as these attributes may also be ours, we are invited to see ourselves as having them only in and through him.

In particular, the attributes of the faithful are ours by grace (objectively) before they become ours by faith and works of love (subjectively). Because by grace Jesus has made us his own, we by faith are called to make him our own. As we receive him, we are enabled to live lives of love in conformity and witness to him. Because these attributes are his, they are also appointed to be ours as well—first as a gift, then as a task (or in the case of persecution, as a matter of historical and providential contingency). Our task is then to become in ourselves what we already are in him.

As he appoints us to be merciful, pure in heart, peacemakers, and persecuted, he does not leave us desolate. He is present in the power of the Spirit, who as the Spirit of Christ is the foretaste of the promised future. Our lives are lived here and now in the presence of Jesus Christ, and our future is the future of Jesus Christ.

On the matter of the wideness of God's mercy—of the two concentric circles as centered in Christ—full weight needs to be accorded to Romans 11:32, which states, "For God has consigned all to disobedience, that he may have mercy on all."

This statement, taken as it stands, seems to suggest that the circle of divine mercy will be no less wide than the circle of human disobedience—note how the word *all* appears twice—and that it is mercy that prevails over disobedience. This seems to be the definitive statement of the Apostle's hope, although questions are left open. Paul can take his thoughts no further, breaking off into the language of doxology (Rom 11:33–36).

If this were the only statement in the New Testament about our ultimate hope, we would all need to be universalists. And in the New Testament, Romans 11:32 does not stand alone in this vein. As we have seen, there are other passages that complement it. Nevertheless, there are also well-known passages pointing in a very different direction.

These different sets of passages, taken as a whole, are best allowed to stand in unresolved tension. Nevertheless, we have solid exegetical and theological grounds for believing that the wrath of God against "all ungodliness and wickedness" (Rom 1:18) is the penultimate and not the ultimate word. The last word belongs to God's grace toward lost sinners—in and through Jesus Christ.

If God's love in Christ extends to all, then we are enjoined to pray and hope that finally no one will be lost. The very passage where we read that "God our Savior...desires all people to be saved and to come to the knowledge of the truth" (1 Tim 2:3–4) is preceded with an apostolic call to prayer: "First of all, then, I urge that supplications, prayers, intercessions, and thanksgivings be made for all people" (1 Tim 2:1).

A telling example from liturgical practice may be taken from the *Catechism of the Catholic Church*. While the idea of universal salvation is explicitly rejected (para. 1035), room is still left for hopeful prayer.

> 1037 In the Eucharistic liturgy and in the daily prayers of her faithful, the Church implores the mercy of God, who does not want "any to perish, but all to come to repentance." (2 Pet 3:9)

> 1058 The Church prays that no one should be lost: "Lord, let me never be parted from you." If it is true that no one can save himself, it is also true that God "desires all men to be saved" (1 Tim 2:4), and that for him "all things are possible" (Mt 19:26).

> 1821 We can therefore hope in the glory of heaven promised by God to those who love him and do his will. In every circumstance, each one of us should hope, with the grace of God, to persevere "to the end" and to obtain the joy of heaven, as God's eternal reward for the good works accomplished with the grace of Christ. In hope, the Church prays for "all men to be saved."

The rejection of universalism as a matter of doctrine, while preserving the spirit of universal hope in liturgical prayer, would seem an admirable way of maintaining the proper stance. It is a posture of tension, humility, and openness in relation to the future of God.[2]

We have the promise that all things will be made new (Rev 21:5), but we do not know exactly what "all things" includes. We have a well-founded hope in God's mercy, without knowing how wide the circle of mercy will be.

> After this I looked, and behold, [I saw] a great multitude that no one could number, from every nation, from all tribes and peoples and languages, standing before the throne and before the Lamb, clothed in white robes, with palm branches in their hands. (Rev 7:9)

Passages like this one make the circle seem very wide indeed, certainly much wider than the dominant tradition has supposed. What could be wider than a promised future filled by so great a multitude that it exceeds the human capacity to number it? What could be more inclusive than every nation, with all tribes and peoples and languages in the throng?[3]

It is this same wideness of mercy that we have found in the Beatitudes. All the faithful of the Beatitudes are needy, and it is the hope of the praying church that each and every one of the world's needy—itself a great multitude beyond number—will at last be counted among the faithful who know and acknowledge Christ for who he is.

The Christ who stands at the center of both the inner and the outer circles is the Christ who establishes the periphery—and his kingdom will have no end. The kingdom of heaven that he promised is not only eternal in duration but also infinite in scope.

STUDY GUIDE QUESTIONS

Prepared by Katherine M. Douglass

These questions are written for personal or group reflection.

THE NEEDY

1. How would you describe your "needs"? Are they financial, physical, emotional? How are these different than "wants"?
2. Have you ever thought of yourself as "needing" the cross or "needing" Christ? How might this perspective on your relationship with Christ add to your understanding of him?
3. In what ways might your needs be a witness to Christ?
4. In what ways is it a comfort to know that Jesus is "God with us" in our suffering or need?
5. What are the signs of Jesus' presence that you have experienced in times of need?

CHAPTER ONE: BLESSED ARE THE POOR IN SPIRIT,
FOR THEIRS IS THE KINGDOM OF HEAVEN.

1. Have you ever felt abandoned by God and felt like crying out, "My God, why have you forsaken me?" When was that moment, and what events led up to it? What followed? If you have not experienced this, what experience might lead you to feel this way?
2. Do you agree that the "poor in spirit" are a restricted group (that group being limited to people of faith)? Why or why not?
3. The kingdom of God is described as the ultimate reality. How would you define the relationship between what is "real" and

"ultimate reality"? Have you ever experienced what you would identify as the kingdom of God, or ultimate reality breaking into reality?

4. Which of the statistics about poverty surprise you most, those about the world or the United States?

5. Physical and financial gifts are described as "material spirituality." Take a moment to meditate on this phrase. What does your material spirituality look like in your life, as an individual or as a part of a congregation?

6. Which of the following do you think is the cause of our apathy regarding the poor? Or perhaps, you think there is something else? Having considered these excuses, what might transform your apathy into action?

    a. Perhaps you feel overwhelmed by statistics about national and world poverty?

    b. Do you question whether financial giving only enables cycles of poverty?

    c. Have you seen the poor squander money?

    d. Do you think that it is the government rather than individuals who are more responsible to care for the poor?

    e. Perhaps you feel that Jesus' statement that "You always have the poor with you" justifies inaction.

CHAPTER TWO: BLESSED ARE THOSE WHO MOURN, FOR THEY SHALL BE COMFORTED.

1. Can you recall a time when you ought to have mourned?

2. Do you know of anyone who "mourns well" or properly? How is their mourning embodied?

3. We usually think of mourning as related to grief. Have you ever mourned for your own sins?

4. A ministry of comfort for those who mourn is described as being "present in a supportive way." Have you ever experienced this kind of comfort? How would you describe the way in which you were comforted?

5. What opportunities do you have this week to mourn with others or to listen deeply to them?

6. Where are the spaces where you are able to mourn your own sins or lament of your own circumstances?
7. What are the barriers to lamenting? Is it scary to imagine bringing anger to God? Would naming a "sin" in an act of mourning be too painful or too real?

CHAPTER THREE: BLESSED ARE THE MEEK, FOR THEY SHALL INHERIT THE EARTH.

1. Which of the three examples of meekness at the beginning of the chapter resonates most with you?
2. What do you think about Brother Lawrence's "holy nonchalance" toward his personal sins? How might this disposition give real priority to Jesus Christ? What is the scariest dimension of holding this kind of disposition toward sin?
3. At the end of his life, Brother Lawrence told the truth, that he was in pain, but he did so without complaint. How is he a model for both living and dying as a witness to Jesus Christ?
4. In your own words, how would you describe the difference between treating things as having intrinsic versus instrumental value? How might you do this with your family and friends? How might you do this in your relationship with God?
5. Under what circumstances would you be willing to become poor in a manner similar to Dorothy Day?
6. The kind of selfless commitment to a cause that Day embodied is rare. Do you think that this is the kind of poverty or meekness that Christ calls each of us to? If so, what blocks us from living in solidarity with the poor? If not, what kind of meekness or poverty is Christ then calling us to?

CHAPTER FOUR: BLESSED ARE THOSE WHO HUNGER AND THIRST FOR RIGHTEOUSNESS, FOR THEY SHALL BE SATISFIED.

1. What are some immediate ways that you might begin to participate in the Holy Spirit's work of addressing environmental unrighteousness?
   a. How might you reduce energy consumption in your home?

    b. Where could you walk or bike or take public transportation that you currently drive?

    c. Would buying organic groceries or starting a backyard garden be one way of resisting the use of pesticides and fertilizer that have become so prevalent in industrial farming in the United States?

    d. Do you know of any local farmers from whom to purchase organic vegetables and meat?

2. What kinds of righteousness do you hunger and thirst for? How do you seek to satisfy these through your own activism?

3. What can you do to adopt a sustainable lifestyle and help create resilient communities?

THE FAITHFUL

1. According to the Beatitudes, the faithful are described as merciful, pure in heart, peacemakers, and objects of persecution for righteousness' sake. How would you describe the faithful today? In what ways is your definition in harmony or tension with this description?

2. At this midway point, how would you describe Jesus as being both a promise and blessing in the Beatitudes?

CHAPTER FIVE: BLESSED ARE THE MERCIFUL, FOR THEY SHALL RECEIVE MERCY.

1. Have you ever seen Jesus act in and through you? Describe when and where this happened. How did you know God was present?

2. What are your thoughts about universal salvation, or the possibility of the salvation of all of humanity? If you were to describe what your beliefs were as a child, then as a teenager, then as a young adult, and then now, how would you describe the way your views have changed or stayed the same? What were the key teachings, or who were the key figures that shaped your beliefs?

3. Who do you know, right now, who is in need of your mercy? In what situations might you offer vertical or horizontal mercy? What do you think happens to justice and righteous anger when mercy prevails?
4. Have you ever received mercy upon showing mercy to another person? Or have you ever been the recipient of mercy? How did that experience affect you?

CHAPTER SIX: BLESSED ARE THE PURE IN HEART, FOR THEY SHALL SEE GOD.

1. We often think about baptism as something that happens once, usually near the birth of a baby. How might baptismal washing, that leads to purity of heart, be something that marks your life?
2. Do you know of anyone who you would describe as "pure in heart"? What characteristics do they have that lead you to give them this description?
3. What changes might you see in your life that would be evidence of being transformed into the likeness of Jesus Christ?

CHAPTER SEVEN: BLESSED ARE THE PEACEMAKERS, FOR THEY SHALL BE CALLED CHILDREN OF GOD.

1. What are the challenges of believing that Christ is the motivating source of all true peacemaking in a pluralistic world (i.e., a world full of people of different beliefs)? Do you think it is best to keep beliefs like this a secret or to talk openly and respectfully about them? How might your familiarity with a person influence your choice?
2. We often talk about Christians being the "children of God," but not necessarily in connection to being peacemakers. How has this section informed your thinking about the role of peacemaking and reconciliation with regard to your own identity as a child of God?
3. If you were to identify one area of your own life where you would like to see more peace, where would that be? What

would be the first signs of peace beginning to influence this place?

CHAPTER EIGHT: BLESSED ARE THOSE
WHO ARE PERSECUTED FOR RIGHTEOUSNESS' SAKE,
FOR THEIRS IS THE KINGDOM OF HEAVEN.

1. Have you ever had the opportunity to participate in nonviolent protest? If so, what motivated your decision to participate?
2. Would you consider yourself to be a pacifist? If so, do you find it easier to be a pacifist in theory than in practice? If not, what prevents you from identifying as one?
3. Having read this section, how would you describe the difference between suffering and persecution? Have you ever experienced either? Would you describe these experiences differently now, with these freshly defined terms?
4. Who are people who are persecuted in your community? What might you do to intervene in their situation?

CHAPTER NINE: BLESSED ARE YOU WHEN OTHERS REVILE
YOU AND PERSECUTE YOU AND UTTER ALL KINDS
OF EVIL AGAINST YOU FALSELY ON MY ACCOUNT.
REJOICE AND BE GLAD, FOR YOUR REWARD IS
GREAT IN HEAVEN, FOR SO THEY PERSECUTED
THE PROPHETS WHO WERE BEFORE YOU.

1. What would your reaction be today if you were to hear someone claim to be God, or to have to same status as God?
2. What words or actions do we consider to be blasphemous today?
3. A common response to remembering those whom the church has killed is to say, "Well, it wasn't *me* who killed them." How might we participate in a form of remembrance that asks for forgiveness and seeks reconciliation in a way that offers

authentic remorse and claims appropriate responsibility? Various governments have issued apologies to groups of people; for example, the Canadian government offered an apology to the native people for treating them harshly and taking their land. What is your reaction to these kinds of apologies? How might they be a secular example to the kind of reconciliation that Christ calls us to?

4. Some denominations use the language of sins of "commission" and sins of "omission." The former refer to the sins we actively commit, the latter refers to the sin we commit by what we have not done. Sins of commission are often easier to confess than sins of omission. How might you become aware of your sins of omission, as an individual or as a congregation? What friends, family members, ministers, or perhaps even journalists do you trust to help you become aware of your sins of omission?

NOTES

INTRODUCTION

1. Pope Benedict XVI, *Jesus of Nazareth: From the Baptism in the Jordan to the Transfiguration*, trans. Adrian J. Walker (San Francisco: Ignatius Press, 2008), 74.

CHAPTER ONE

1. Dietrich Bonhoeffer, *Discipleship*, ed. Geffrey B. Kelly and John D. Godsey, trans. Barbara Green and Reinhard Krauss (Minneapolis: Augsburg Fortress, 2001), 101. (Further page references in the text.)

2. Bonhoeffer, *Letters and Papers from Prison*, ed. John W. de Gruchy, trans. Isabel Best et al. (Minneapolis: Augsburg Fortress, 2010), 361 (translation revised.)

3. "The Last Written Words of Luther," Table Talk No. 5468, (16 February 1546), in *Dr. Martin Luthers Werke* (1909) Band 85 (TR 5), as translated by James A. Kellerman, 317–18.

4. All statistics in this section taken from Anup Shah, "Poverty Facts and Stats," http://www.globalissues.org/article /26/poverty-facts-and-stats. Last updated September 2010. Further documentation may be found at this website.

5. UNICEF, "The Progress of Nations 2000," http://www .unicef.org/pon00/immu1.htm.

6. The figures in this section are taken from the University of Michigan's National Poverty Center. Further documentation may be found at their website: http://www.npc.umich.edu/poverty/.

7. "The World Distribution of Household Wealth" 2006, 72 pp., a report issued by the World Institute for Development Economics

Research of the United Nations University (UNU-WIDER), http://www.iariw.org/papers/2006/davies.pdf.

8. Press Release: "Pioneering Study Shows Richest Own Half World Wealth," Global Policy Forum, December 5, 2006, http://www.globalpolicy.org/component/content/article/218/46555.html.

9. See, for example, The Global Poverty Project, http://www.globalpovertyproject.com/pages/about_us.

10. See also Jeffrey D. Sachs, *The End of Poverty: Economic Possibilities for Our Time* (New York: Penguin Press, 2005).

11. Zildo Rocha, *Helder, O Dom* (Petrópolis, Rio de Janeiro: Editora Vozes, 2000), 53.

12. Similar efforts at outreach and reciprocity might also be organized, of course, to include other ecclesial bodies like the Eastern Orthodox and the Pentecostals.

13. I do not mean to suggest that poverty of this magnitude can be met only by efforts of the church. National and international governmental and nongovernmental interventions are also obviously necessary. Christians more alert to the needs of the global poor could be a catalyst for the needed interventions, as many of them (though not enough) already have been.

Chapter Two

1. Jesus mourns "against" them in the sense that he laments when they fail to mourn for the right things, in the right way, and at the right time.

2. Cf. Athanasius, "Letters to Serapion on the Holy Spirit," in *Athanasius*, ed. Khaled Anatolios (London: Routledge, 2004), 220.

3. Roman Catholic and Eastern Orthodox Christians, of course, have institutionalized forms by which sins may be confessed to a priest, and by which repentance and forgiveness are included in the eucharist. Protestant Christians, who lack the concreteness of these traditions, may nonetheless confess their sins in daily prayer, in public worship, and in intimate conversations with other Christians.

4. Deborah van Deusen Hunsinger, *Pray Without Ceasing: Revitalizing Pastoral Care* (Grand Rapids, MI: Wm. B. Eerdmans, 2006), 138.

5. Claus Westermann, "The Role of Lament in the Theology of the Old Testament," *Interpretation* 28 (1974): 20–38, on 26.

6. For a visual display of how this psalm also exhibits a chiasmic structure, see Hunsinger, *Pray Without Ceasing*, 143.

7. Hughes Oliphant Old, *Leading in Prayer: Workbook for Worship* (Grand Rapids, MI: Wm. B. Eerdmans, 1995), 80. Quoted by Hunsinger, *Pray Without Ceasing*, 144.

8. Personal communication from Thomas M. Crisp, Associate Professor of Philosophy at Biola University, April 2012.

9. Matt Talbot, "I Was Hungry," *Vox Nova* (blog), April 18, 2012, http://vox-nova.com/2012/04/18/i-was-hungry/.

CHAPTER THREE

1. Dietrich Bonhoeffer, *Ethics*, trans. Neville Horton Smith (New York: Touchstone, 1995), 135–37.

2. *The Practice of the Presence of God: Critical Edition*, ed. Conrad de Meester (Washington, D.C.: Institute of Carmelite Studies, 1994). (Page references cited in the text.)

3. One remarkable story had to do with his being sent to Burgundy to fetch wine for the priory. This was a painful task for him. Not only did he know nothing about wine, but his leg was crippled and he could only get about on the boat by dragging himself over the barrels. Yet he did not worry about it or about the purchase of the wine. He turned the problem over to God, after which he discovered that all was accomplished, and all was done well! He had been sent to Auvergne the previous year for the same reason. He could not explain how everything worked out as well as it did, since he did not believe that he was the one who accomplished it. (Ibid., 92–93, revised trans.)

4. Ibid., xxxvii.

5. Ibid., xlvi, n. 84.

6. For a description of the rigors of convent life, see Dorothy Day, *Therese* (Springfield, IL: Templegate Publishers, 1960), 162; cf. 145.

7. *The Complete Thérèse of Lisieux*, ed. Robert J. Edmondson (Brewster, MA: Paraclete Press, 2009), vii–xxv.

8. Hans Urs von Balthasar, *Two Sisters in the Spirit: Thérèse of Lisieux and Elisabeth of the Trinity*, trans. Donald Nichols, Anne Englund

Nash, and Dennis Martin (San Francisco: Ignatius Press, 1992), 28, 195. Subsequent page references, including two statements by St. Thérèse, in the text.

9. *The Complete Thérèse*, 184–85.

10. Ibid., p. 59.

11. Quoted by Conrad de Meester, *With Empty Hands: The Message of Thérèse of Lisieux* (Washington, D.C.: ICS Publications, 2002), 123.

12. Balthasar, *Two Sisters*, 95, 283–84; de Meester, *With Empty Hands*, 124.

13. Quoted by de Meester, *With Empty Hands*, 136.

14. *The Complete Thérèse*, 231, 235. These are the final words in her autobiographical reflections, "The Story of a Soul," completed shortly before her death.

15. As cited in Dorothy Day, *Thérèse*, 165–66 (see n27). For a different translation, see *The Complete Thérèse*, 261.

16. See *The Practice of the Presence of God*, ed. Donald Attwater (Springfield, IL: Templegate, 1974), and Day, *Thérèse* (see n27).

17. David J. O'Brien, "The Pilgrimage of Dorothy Day," *Commonweal*, December 19, 1980, 711–15, on 711.

18. Day, introduction to Attwater, *The Practice of the Presence of God*, 17–18, 19 (see n37).

19. Day, *On Pilgrimage* (Grand Rapids, MI: Wm. B. Eerdmans, 1999), 110. Despite the apparent centrality of Brother Lawrence to Day's spiritual practices, he receives little or no attention in the biographies written about her.

20. Day, *Selected Writings: By Little and By Little*, ed. Robert Ellsberg (Maryknoll, NY: Orbis, 1993), 285.

21. Day, *On Pilgrimage*, 42.

22. Day, "Inventory—January 1951," *The Catholic Worker*, January 1951. *The Catholic Worker Movement*, http://dorothyday .catholicworker.org/articles/195.html.

23. *All the Way to Heaven: Selected Letters of Dorothy Day*, ed. Robert Ellsberg (Maryknoll, NY: Orbis, 2011), 470.

24. Day, *Loaves and Fishes* (NY: Orbis, 1963), 71, 82.

25. Quoted in Jim Forest, *All Is Grace: A Biography of Dorothy Day* (Maryknoll, NY: Orbis, 2011), 166.

CHAPTER FOUR

1. Bonhoeffer, *Discipleship*, ed. Geffrey B. Kelly and John D. Godsey, trans. Barbara Green and Reinhard Krauss (Minneapolis: Augsburg Fortress, 2001), 106 (see n2).

2. See Eberhard Bethge, *Dietrich Bonhoeffer: A Biography*, ed. Edwin Robertson, trans. Eric Mosbacher et al., rev. ed. (Minneapolis: Augsburg Fortress, 2000), 176.

3. Steven Mithen, "Freedom through Cooking," *New York Review of Books*, October 22, 2009. According to a distinguished scientist at Cambridge University, the human race has only a 50/50 chance of surviving another century. See Sir Martin Rees, *Our Final Hour: A Scientist's Warning; How Terror, Error, and Environmental Disaster Threaten Humankind's Future in This Century—On Earth and Beyond* (NY: Basic Books, 2003).

4. George F. Kennan, *Democracy and the Student Left* (New York: Bantam Books, 1968), 229–30.

5. Jack F. Matlock, "George F. Kennan," *Proceedings of the American Philosophical Society* 151 (June 2001): 233–42, on 242.

6. All churches would do well to learn from groups like the Mennonite Creation Care Network: http://mennocreationcare.org.

7. Walter Russell Mead, "Christianity Becomes Global Religious Superpower," *The Feed* (blog), *The American Interest*, December 21, 2011, http://blogs.the-american-interest.com/wrm/2011/12/20/the-missionaries-win-christianity-becomes-global-religious-superpower/?.

8. See Bay Localize, "Community Resilience Toolkit 2.0," www.baylocalize.org/toolkit.

9. Bioneers website: http://www.bioneers.org/.

10. Transition Network website: http://transitionnetwork .org/.

11. Resilience Alliance website: http://www.resalliance.org/.

12. In a well-functioning democracy, plans like these would receive large government subsidies to implement them on the widest possible scale. Unfortunately, as Jimmy Carter commented in July 2013, the United States is no longer a functioning democracy.

13. John Robb, "Why Financial Collapse Is Only the Beginning: Six Rules to Live By to Protect your Family." Online report available at: http://www.resilientcommunities.com/.

14. "About John Robb," http://globalguerrillas.typepad.com /about.html.

15. Wendell Berry, "17 Rules for a Sustainable Local Community," presented on November 11, 1994, at the 23rd annual meeting of the Northern Plains Resource Council. The essay is widely available on the internet.

CHAPTER FIVE

1. See Wendell Berry's story, "Pray Without Ceasing," in *Fidelity: Five Stories* (New York: Pantheon, 1992).

2. *The Study Catechism, Full Version* (Louisville, KY: Witherspoon Press, 1998), 30 (question 49).

3. Timothy Ware, *The Orthodox Church*, new ed. (London: Penguin Books, 1997), 262.

4. Thomas F. Torrance, "Universalism or Election?," *Scottish Journal of Theology* 2 (1949): 310–18, on 313, 314.

5. Hans Urs von Balthasar, *Dare We Hope "That All Men Be Saved?,"* trans. David Kipp and Lothar Krauth (San Francisco: Ignatius Press, 1988), 187 (translation revised). Balthasar's convictions are similar on this point to those of Henri de Lubac, Jean Daniélou, and Joseph Ratzinger. See Nicholas J. Healy, *The Eschatology of Hans Urs von Balthasar* (Oxford: Oxford University Press, 2005), 206.

6. St. Thérèse, we might note, once wrote a Christmas play for her sisters, in which the Child Jesus insists, while correcting the Angel of Vengeance, that, "every soul will find forgiveness." On the last day, the Child Jesus will remain "the God of love" whose sufferings are enough to compensate for all the sins of the entire human race. See *Poems of St. Teresa, Carmelite of Lisieux*, trans. S. L. Emery (Boston: Carmelite Convent, 1907).

7. F. Kefa Sempangi, *A Distant Grief: The Real Story behind the Martyrdom of Christians in Uganda* (Glendale, CA: Regal Books, 1979), 119–20. These stories do not always have a happy ending. Sempangi's friend and convert, Joseph Kiwanuka, founder of the Ugandan

National Congress and a leader in the congregation, was hunted down, tortured, and brutally murdered by the same forces (56–60, 172–73). See also Sempangi, *From the Dust: A Sequel to A Distant Grief* (Eugene, OR: Wipf and Stock, 2008).

8. Orlando Costas, "The Subversiveness of Faith," *Ecumenical Review* (1988): 66–78; on p. 73.

9. Tomás Borge, *Christianity and Revolution: Tomás Borge's Theology of Life*, ed. and trans. Andrew Reding (Maryknoll, NY: Orbis, 1987), 23–24.

10. Borge, *Christianity and Revolution*, v. (Co-written with Luis Enrique Meja Gody, translation revised.)

11. *Merchant of Venice*, act 4, scene 1.

CHAPTER SIX

1. Jonathan Edwards, "The Pure in Heart Blessed," in *The Works of Jonathan Edwards*, vol. 17, ed. Mark Valeri (New Haven: Yale University Press, 1999), 57–86, on 64.

2. See Suzanne McDonald, "Beholding God's Glory: John Owen and the 'Reforming' of the Beatific Vision," in *The Ashgate Companion to John Owen*, ed. Kelly Kapic and Mark Jones (Aldershot, UK: Ashgate, 2012).

3. E. L. Mascall, *Corpus Christi: Essays on the Church and the Eucharist* (London: Longmans, Green and Co., 1953), 30–31.

CHAPTER SEVEN

1. Athanasius, *On the Incarnation* (London: Geoffrey Bles, The Centenary Press, 1944), 91. (References hereafter in the text.)

2. Karl Barth, *Church Dogmatics*, vol. IV, part 2, ed. G. W. Bromiley and T. F. Torrance (Edinburgh: T & T Clark, 1958), 550. (References to this volume are hereafter cited in the text as IV/2.)

3. For further examples and discussion, see Glen H. Stassen, *Just Peacemaking: Transforming Initiatives for Justice and Peace* (Louisville, KY: Westminster John Knox Press, 1992).

4. See *Improving School Climate: Schools Implementing Restorative Practices* (International Institute for Restorative Practices, 2009), 1–36,

on 6–8, http://www.realjustice.org/pdf /IIRP-Improving-School-Climate .pdf.

5. See Daniel W. Van Ness and Karen Heetderks Strong, *Restoring Justice: An Introduction to Restorative Justice*, 4th ed. (New Providence, NJ: Matthew Bender and Co., 2010); Howard Zehr, *Justpeace Ethics: A Guide to Restorative Justice and Peacebuilding* (Eugene, OR: Cascade Books, 2009).

6. Barth, *Church Dogmatics*, vol. II, part 1, ed. G. W. Bromiley and T. F. Torrance (Edinburgh: T & T Clark, 1957), 397. (Hereafter cited as II/1 in the text.)

Chapter Eight

1. See, however, Luke 13:31, which reads, "At that very hour some Pharisees came and said to him, 'Get away from here, for Herod wants to kill you.'"

2. Anthony Trollope, *The Warden* (New York: Oxford University Press, 1980 [1952]). Hereafter page references cited in the text.

3. From Webb Miller, *I Found No Peace: The Journal of a Foreign Correspondent* (New York: Simon and Schuster, 1936), 193–95.

4. See Peter Ackerman and Jack DuVall, *A Force More Powerful: A Century of Non-Violent Conflict* (New York: Palgrave Macmillan, 2001); Gene Sharp, *Waging Nonviolent Struggle: 20th Century Practice and 21st Century Potential* (Boston: Porter Sargent, 2005).

Chapter Nine

1. Barth, *The Göttingen Dogmatics: Instruction in the Christian Religion*, ed. Hannelotte Reiffen, trans. G. W. Bromiley (Grand Rapids, MI: Wm. B. Eerdmans, 1990), 153.

2. For a discussion of blasphemy as a charge against Jesus and an assessment of its historicity, see Raymond E. Brown, *The Death of the Messiah*, vol. 1 (New York: Doubleday, 1994), 516–47. For the objection (and its dismissal as "very weak indeed") that Jesus could not have been accused of blasphemy because he was not stoned to death (as Stephen would be later on), see 532–34. See also Darrell L. Bock, *Blasphemy and Exaltation in Judaism and the Final Examination of Jesus* (Tübingen: Mohr Siebeck, 1998).

3. Among recent New Testament scholars whose work supports the faith of the church in such matters, we might mention Raymond E. Brown, Nils A. Dahl, Martin Hengel, J. Louis Martyn, Beverly Roberts Gaventa, Joseph A. Fitzmyer, N. T. Wright, Otfried Hofius, I. Howard Marshall, Richard B. Hays, Marcus Brockmuhl, Marianne Meye Thompson, Richard Bauckham, and many others.

4. Søren Kierkegaard, *Practice in Christianity*, ed. Howard V. Hong and Edna H. Hong (Princeton, NJ: Princeton University Press, 1991), 81.

5. David B., Barrett, et al., *World Christian Encyclopedia: A Comparative Survey of Churches and Religions in the Modern World*, 2nd. ed. (New York: Oxford University Press, 2001), 227–29.

6. "Status of Global Mission, 2010," *International Bulletin of Missionary Research* 34, no. 1.

7. All numbers of martyrs in the text are henceforth taken from the *World Christian Database*: http://www.worldchristiandatabase.org/wcd/.

8. The Voice of the Martyrs, "China," http://www.persecution.net/china.htm. For the figure of 130 million, see "Sons of Heaven: Inside China's Fastest-growing Non-governmental Organisation," *The Economist*, October 2, 2008.

9. C. E. B. Cranfield, *1 & 2 Peter and Jude* (London: SCM Press, 1960), 120.

10. "St. Patrick's Breastplate," words attributed to St. Patrick (372–466); trans. Cecil Frances Alexander, 1889.

11. From "Ah, Holy Jesus," written by Johann Heermann (1585–1647).

12. Hans Küng, in *Christians and Jews*, ed. Hans Küng and Walter Kasper (New York: Seabury, 1975), 11–12 (translation revised).

13. Barth, *The Church and the Political Problem of Our Day* (New York: Charles Scribners' Sons, 1939), 51.

14. Wisdom about responsible assistance today can be found in Ronald Boyd-MacMillan, *Faith That Endures: The Essential Guide to the Persecuted Church* (Grand Rapids, MI: Revell, 2006), chap. 4. (Under no circumstances, however, should prayer be spoken of, barbarically, as a "tactic.")

15. See William T. Cavanaugh, *Torture and Eucharist: Theology, Politics, and the Body of Christ* (Oxford: Blackwell Publishers, 1998).

16. *Tertio millennio adveniente* (Apostolic Letter for the Jubilee Year 2000), no. 37.

17. See James H. Cone, *The Cross and the Lynching Tree* (Maryknoll, NY: Orbis, 2011).

18. See "Lynchings: By State and Race, 1882–1968." University of Missouri-Kansas City School of Law. Retrieved 2010-07-26. Statistics provided by the archives at Tuskegee Institute. Cited from Wikipedia article, "Lynching," http://en.wikipedia.org /wiki/Lynching# cite_note-tuskegee_umkc-0.

19. See *Persecuted and Forgotten? A Report on Christians Oppressed for Their Faith* (Sutton, Surry, UK: Aid to the Church in Need, 2011).

CONCLUSION

1. Technically, of course, the word translated as "blessed" (*makarios*) is an adjective. Nevertheless, the term "blessed" is a better translation than "happy," precisely because the term "blessed" makes clear that the unnamed source of the blessing is God. Behind the adjective, we might say, is an implicit divine passive.

2. Similar liturgical prayers for the salvation of all people could of course be cited from other Christian churches and traditions.

3. The wideness of God's mercy, as suggested here, would not necessarily preclude the severity of God's judgment. We do not know exactly how this severity will finally be worked out. But we do know that it was borne by Christ on behalf of us all (Rom 8:3; 2 Cor 5:14), and that God "has consigned all to disobedience, that he may have mercy on all" (Rom 11:32).

LIST OF ILLUSTRATIONS
All works are by
Rembrandt Harmensz van Rijn (1606–69)

THE BEATITUDES

"BLESSED ARE THE MEEK…" p. 29
The Adoration of the Shepherds, around 1654. Musee des Beaux-Arts de la Ville de Paris, Petit Palais.
© Petit Palais, Roger-Viollet, The Image Works. Used with permission.

"BLESSED ARE THOSE WHO HUNGER…" p. 46
Christ driving the Money Changers from the Temple (B. Holl. 69; H. 126), etching with drypoint, 1635
© Christie's Images Limited, 2012. Used with permission.

"THE FAITHFUL" p. 59
Christ Appearing to the Disciples
The Louvre / Bibliothèque nationale de France. Used with permission.

"BLESSED ARE THE MERCIFUL…" p. 61
Jesus Heals a Leper
Courtesy the Rijksmuseum, Amsterdam

"BLESSED ARE THE PURE IN HEART…" p. 72
The Last Supper, after Leonardo da Vinci. 1634–1635. Red chalk, 14 1/4 x 18 11/16 in. (36.2 x 47.5 cm) Robert Lehman Collection, 1975 (1975.1.794)
The Metropolitan Museum of Art
Image copyright © The Metropolitan Museum of Art. Image source: Art Resource, NY. Used with permission.

"BLESSED ARE THE PEACEMAKERS…" p. 80
Christ and the Woman Taken in Adultery
Photo © Hans Thorwid, Courtesy Nationalmuseum, Stockholm. Used with permission.

"BLESSED ARE THOSE WHO ARE PERSECUTED…" p. 93
Christ Taken Before Caiaphas
Courtesy the Cleveland Museum of Art

"THE FINAL WORD" p. 101
The Three Crosses, c. 1653. Found in the collection of the Museum Boijmans Van Beuningen, Rotterdam.
PHOTO CREDIT: HIP, Art Resource, NY. Used with permission.